INA PAARMAN

THE GOOD FOOD
COOKBOOK

THE GOOD FOOD
COOKBOOK

INA PAARMAN

PHOTOGAPHY BY
CRAIG FRASER

Struik Publishers (Pty) Ltd
(a member of Struik New Holland
Publishing (Pty) Ltd)
Cornelis Struik House
80 McKenzie Street
Cape Town 8001

Reg. No.: 54/00965/07

ISBN 1 86872 485 9

First published in 2000
10 9 8 7 6 5 4 3 2

publishing manager: Linda de Villiers
designer: Petal Palmer
design assistant: Lellyn Creamer
editor: Catherine Murray
proofreader and indexer: Brenda
Brickman
photographer: Craig Fraser
food stylist: Justine Kiggen
food stylist's assistants: Elizabeth
Copeland and Janet Hacking

reproduction by Hirt & Carter Cape
(Pty) Ltd
printed and bound by CTP Book
Printers (Pty) Ltd

CONTENTS

microwave courgette soup with feta cheese

'... prize above all else

in the world those who love you

and who wish you well.'

Alexander Solzhenitsyn

SOUPS

MICROWAVE COURGETTE SOUP
WITH FETA CHEESE

SERVES 3–4

*Prepare this soup a day in advance, as the flavour
improves after a day.*

2 cups (500 ml) chicken stock
6–8 small courgettes, quartered
1 small potato, peeled and grated
1 small onion, chopped
1 green pepper, seeded and diced
1–2 cloves garlic, crushed
½ t (2.5 ml) seasoned sea salt
1 bunch chives, chopped
½ cup (125 ml) crumbled feta cheese

Microwave all the ingredients, except the chives and feta
cheese, in a large, covered microwave-safe dish on high
(100 per cent) for 12 minutes, stirring from time to time.
Liquidise, taste for seasoning and add half the chives.

To serve, reheat and garnish with the remaining chives and
feta cheese. Alternatively, serve cold, topped with the feta
cheese and remaining chives.

VARIATIONS

■   Substitute either carrots or Granny Smith apples for the
courgettes. The sharp taste of feta cheese is excellent with
all three variations.

■   For a marbled effect, dish two soups of different colours,
e.g. carrot and courgette, into each soup bowl and garnish
with watercress or mint.

COOK'S TIP
A large microwave-safe dish with a lid is an excellent
investment for soups made in the microwave, or
for steaming vegetables.

COLD AVOCADO SOUP
WITH CORIANDER

SERVES 6

*A memorable pale green, creamy soup. If you are not a
coriander fan, replace it with mint, chives or fresh origanum.
I have a patch of origanum growing in a dry, sunny spot in
my back garden where it seems to thrive on neglect.*

3 large or 4 small ripe avocados, peeled, stoned and
cut into chunks
juice of 1 lime or lemon
few drops Tabasco sauce
1–2 t (5–10 ml) dry sherry
2 cups (500 ml) milk
2 cups (500 ml) plain yoghurt
2 t (10 ml) finely chopped fresh coriander roots and
stems (well rinsed)
seasoned sea salt to taste
fresh, whole coriander leaves to garnish

Place the avocado chunks in a food processor fitted with a steel
blade and sprinkle with lime or lemon juice. Add the remaining
ingredients and process until smooth (you may have to do this
in batches). Refrigerate for at least 1 hour before serving. Serve
in chilled bowls garnished with coriander leaves, or freeze
coriander leaves in ice cubes beforehand and add as a garnish
just before serving.

COOK'S TIP
When you refrigerate the soup,
add the avocado pip to prevent the soup
from discolouring. Remove before serving.

PEA AND BASIL SOUP

SERVES 6

A pale green summer soup scented with basil,
delicious either hot or cold.

2 small onions, peeled and chopped
2 cloves garlic, crushed
4 T (60 ml) butter
2 cups (500 ml) fresh or frozen peas
4 rashers rindless streaky smoked bacon, roughly chopped
1 small firm iceberg lettuce, finely sliced
4 cups (1 litre) chicken or vegetable stock
salt
freshly ground black pepper
1 cup (250 ml) basil leaves
cream

Gently sauté the onion and garlic in butter for 5 minutes without allowing it to colour (a little salt helps to draw out the juices and prevents browning). Add the peas and the bacon and stir to coat them with the butter. Add the lettuce and stock, bring to the boil and simmer for 15–20 minutes. Blend the mixture in a liquidiser or processor. Return the soup to the saucepan, season with salt and pepper and gently reheat.

Set aside 12 of the best basil leaves. Tear the remaining leaves and stir them into the soup. Divide the soup into bowls, add a spoonful of cream and decorate with the whole basil leaves.

CREAM OF SPINACH AND PARSLEY SOUP WITH LEMON CREAM

SERVES 6

This is a deliciously creamy soup, best made
and served on the same day.

2 T (30 ml) butter
2 leeks (most of the green part removed), washed and sliced
2 cloves garlic, crushed
2 T (30 ml) flour
6 cups (1.5 litres) chicken stock
1 bunch spinach, well washed
1 cup (250 ml) parsley sprigs, washed and patted dry
salt
freshly ground black pepper

½ cup (125 ml) cream
2 T (30 ml) lemon juice
good pinch freshly grated nutmeg
pinch salt

Melt the butter in a medium-sized saucepan. Add the leeks, cover, and sweat them until they are soft. Add the garlic and cook for a little longer. Add the flour and blend in well. Slowly pour in the stock, stirring, and bring to the boil. Simmer, covered, for 10 minutes, then tip in the spinach and parsley. Season with salt and freshly ground pepper. Cook for a further 10 minutes, uncovered, and then purée, in batches, in the liquidiser or processor until very smooth. Check the seasoning before serving and gently reheat.

Just before serving, whip the cream, lemon juice, nutmeg and a pinch of salt together until lightly thickened. Divide the soup between 6 hot bowls, and spoon the lemon cream on top.

MICROWAVE CAULIFLOWER
AND BLUE CHEESE SOUP

SERVES 6

I love cauliflower in soup, and this one has a stunning combination of flavours. It is so quick, easy and delicious. It can easily be prepared on the stove, but somehow in this particular recipe the microwave gives a cleaner flavour.

3 T (45 ml) butter
4 T (60 ml) water
4 medium onions, chopped
2 cups (500 ml) cauliflower, broken into small florets
3 T (45 ml) flour
a pinch of grated nutmeg
2 cups (500 ml) chicken stock
100 g blue cheese, crumbled
2 cups (500 ml) full cream milk
freshly ground black pepper

Combine the butter, water, onions and cauliflower in a covered microwave-safe bowl and microwave on high (100 per cent) for 10 minutes. Stir from time to time during cooking. Add the flour and nutmeg and stir in well. Add the chicken stock and microwave, covered, for 5 minutes. Add the blue cheese, reserving a little for garnishing, and liquidise the soup. Add the milk. Taste for seasoning and reheat for 3–4 minutes on high before serving.

Serve in soup bowls topped with freshly ground black pepper and a sprinkling of blue cheese.

CURRIED MUSSEL SOUP
WITH POTATOES AND SAFFRON

SERVES 6

This soup is a variation on the classic combination of potato, leek and onion. To make it into a complete meal, double the quantity of mussel meat or add some cubed, firm white fish.

1 kg mussels, scrubbed, rinsed and beards removed
1 wineglass dry white wine
4 T (60 ml) butter
1–2 t (5–10 ml) medium-strength curry powder
4 leeks, finely sliced
3 medium potatoes, peeled and diced
1 bay leaf
5 cups (1.25 litre) fish or vegetable stock
½ t (2.5 ml) saffron threads
small bunch chives, snipped (to garnish)
freshly ground black pepper

Place the cleaned mussels into a large pan with the wine. Cover and cook over a fierce heat, shaking the pan a few times, until the mussels open. This takes about 5 minutes. Place a colander over a bowl and tip out the mussels, taking care not to spill any of the liquid.

Melt the butter in a spacious pan and stir in the curry powder, leeks and potatoes. Cook gently for 5 minutes, stirring a couple of times. Strain the mussel liquid through muslin or a fine sieve into the pan with the vegetables, add the bay leaf and stock and bring to the boil. Stir in the saffron and leave to simmer for about 25 minutes.

While the soup simmers, discard the shells from most of the mussels, and remove one half of the shell of the remaining mussels to use in the soup. Stir in the shelled and unshelled mussels, reheat and check the seasoning.

Serve with a sprinkling of chives and ground black pepper.

curried mussel soup with potatoes and saffron

roasted cherry tomato soup

ROASTED CHERRY TOMATO SOUP

SERVES 6

This soup is delicious served cold on a hot summer's day.

600 g ripe cherry tomatoes
3 t (15 ml) garlic and herb seasoning
1 T (15 ml) sugar
2 slices white bread
1 small onion, quartered
3 cloves garlic, crushed
1 small red pepper, seeded and quartered
½ English cucumber, peeled and roughly chopped
1 T (15 ml) lemon juice or cider vinegar
1 T (15 ml) chopped fresh basil, or 1 t (5 ml) dried
3 T (45 ml) cold-pressed, extra virgin olive oil
seasoning to taste
3 x 200 ml tins tomato cocktail

1 cup (250 ml) crushed ice
1 bunch spring onions with green tops, finely sliced
½ English cucumber, unpeeled and finely diced

Preheat the oven to 200 °C. Slice the tomatoes in half and place them cut side up in a roasting pan. Season with garlic and herb seasoning and sugar. Bake uncovered for 30 minutes.

Remove the tomatoes from the oven and process them with the remaining ingredients until completely smooth. If the food processor is over-full, reserve 1 can tomato cocktail and add it later. Taste for seasoning. The flavour must be quite strong as ice cubes and garnishes are added just before serving, which will dilute the taste. Cover with clingfilm and refrigerate.

Prepare the spring onions and cucumber for garnishing and refrigerate in individual bowls.

To serve, add the crushed ice to the soup and hand around bowls of vegetable garnish for your guests to help themselves.

COOK'S TIPS

• Top quality cold-pressed, extra virgin olive oil is a must in this recipe as it enhances the flavour of the dish and gives it an authentic Mediterranean flavour.
• Crush ice by placing the cubes in a clean tea towel and crushing with a wooden mallet.

OXTAIL SOUP WITH A DIFFERENCE

SERVES 6

4 T (60 ml) Canola or sunflower oil
1 kg oxtail
1 large onion, chopped
4 medium carrots, diced
2 sticks celery, sliced
8 cups (2 litres) beef stock
1 bouquet garni (sprig fresh thyme, parsley stalks and
a bay leaf tied together)
5 cm piece fresh ginger cut into julienne strips
fresh coriander

Warm half the oil in a heavybased saucepan and brown the oxtail, then transfer the meat to a plate. Discard the used oil, but don't wash the saucepan. Add the remaining oil to the pan and gently cook the prepared vegetables until they are lightly coloured. Add the stock, oxtail and bouquet garni. Bring to the boil and simmer for 2–3 hours, skimming the fat off occasionally. If you simmer it very gently and skim carefully, there is no need to chill the soup to remove the surface fat, although this is an alternative.

Add the julienne of fresh ginger and some fresh coriander leaves to the soup and serve with country-style bread and a tossed salad to follow.

rich man's cape-style avocado ritz

'Strange to see how a good dinner and

feasting reconciles everybody.'

Samuel Pepys

STARTERS

RICH MAN'S
CAPE-STYLE AVOCADO RITZ

SERVES 8

4 ripe avocados, cut in half, peeled and stoned
lite French dressing
200 g smoked snoek or angelfish carefully boned, skinned
and flaked
a handful of watercress

SEAFOOD SAUCE
½ cup (125 ml) mayonnaise
1 t (5 ml) tomato pesto or tomato paste
1 T (15 ml) brandy
6 drops Tabasco sauce
½ cup (125 ml) cream, whipped
seasoning to taste

200 g smoked salmon trout
1 crayfish tail, cooked and sliced into medallions
salad greens

Slice the avocados and brush lightly with the French dressing to prevent discoloration.

Mix all the ingredients for the seafood sauce. Add flaked snoek or angelfish and taste for seasoning.

Arrange avocado on individual plates with salmon, crayfish, and the dressed snoek or angelfish. Garnish with salad greens and serve.

SMOKED OSTRICH

SERVES 8

South African flavours at their best. Most good delicatessens and speciality butchers stock smoked ostrich. It is best to buy it freshly sliced rather than vacuum packed.

300–400 g smoked ostrich, finely sliced
extra virgin olive oil
freshly ground black pepper
8 T (120 ml) quince jelly
fresh rocket leaves

Fan the ostrich slices carpaccio-style on individual dinner plates. Cover with clingfilm pushed down flat onto the meat. Refrigerate until serving time.

When ready to serve, remove clingfilm from plates. Drizzle olive oil lightly over the meat and season with freshly ground black pepper. Serve with a tablespoon of quince jelly on the side. Garnish with rocket leaves.

VARIATION

Use smoked beef or left-over braaied sirloin, thinly sliced, in place of ostrich. Garnish with flakes of parmesan cheese.

SNOEK PÂTÉ WITH A DIFFERENCE

SERVES 8

The potato in this recipe mellows the strong flavour of the snoek. Don't be shy with the black pepper.

3 medium potatoes
250 g smoked snoek
1 T (15 ml) Balsamic vinegar
2 t (10 ml) tomato pesto or tomato paste
½ t (2.5 ml) sugar
freshly ground black pepper
3 cloves garlic, crushed
½ cup (125 ml) olive oil

Boil and mash the potatoes. Remove the skin and bones and flake the fish. Blend all the ingredients in a food processor. Taste and adjust the seasoning. The pâté has a fridge life of 3 days and should not be frozen. If you prefer a pinker colour, increase the tomato pesto or paste to 2½ t (12.5 ml).

VARIATION
Replace the smoked snoek with 1 x 200 g tin salmon or 250 g smoked salmon offcuts.

COOK'S TIP
For a delicious cocktail snack, heap the pâté onto halved, cooked baby potatoes and top with a sprig of fennel. To make a dip, thin it out with a little milk.

CALAMARI SALAD WITH CORIANDER MAYONNAISE

SERVES 6

It is worth taking the time to tenderise the calamari. Meat tenderiser is made from a natural substance found in papinos.

500 g clean calamari tubes, sliced into rings
meat tenderiser
4 cloves garlic, crushed
1 bay leaf
½ lemon, sliced
½–1 red chilli, sliced, with seeds
½ cup (125 ml) vegetable stock
4 T (60 ml) olive oil
½ cup (125 ml) stoned, sliced black olives
sun-dried tomato quarters
watercress or baby lettuce
1 bunch fresh coriander

Sprinkle the calamari lightly with meat tenderiser. Leave to stand for 20 minutes in a colander. Rinse well and shake dry.

Place the calamari in a saucepan with the garlic, bay leaf, lemon, chilli and vegetable stock. Bring to the boil and immediately remove from the heat. Cover with a lid and allow to stand for 5 minutes to cool in the cooking juices. Drain and toss with the olive oil and olives.

To serve, dish the calamari onto plates and decorate with sun-dried tomato quarters, watercress or lettuce, and coriander leaves (reserve the stems and roots for the coriander mayonnaise). Add a heaped tablespoon of coriander mayonnaise (see recipe overleaf) to each plate.

CORIANDER MAYONNAISE

6 cloves garlic
1 red chilli
stems and roots of 1 bunch coriander, carefully rinsed to
remove all sand
1 egg yolk
about ½ cup (125 ml) Canola or sunflower oil
½ t (2.5 ml) seasoned sea salt
2 T (30 ml) lemon juice

Place the garlic, chilli, coriander stems and roots and egg yolk in
a processor or liquidiser. Process at high speed until fine.
Add the oil very slowly while running the machine, to obtain a
thick mayonnaise. Add the seasoned salt and lemon juice and
mix to blend.

VARIATION
Use dill in place of coriander.

OLIVE PASTE (TAPENADE)

Tapenade is traditionally spread over toasted bread
brushed with olive oil.

1 cup (250 ml) stoned black olives
100 g anchovies, salt cured or 2 x 50 g cans anchovies in oil
2 T (30 ml) capers, drained
4 T (60 ml) olive oil
2 T (30 ml) lemon juice
freshly ground black pepper

Place the olives, anchovies (with their oil) and the capers in a
food processor. Add the olive oil and lemon juice while the
machine is running. Process to a rough-textured paste. Taste
and add pepper.

PRAWNS WITH GARLIC AND CHILLI

SERVES 5–6

This is quick, easy and delicious.

500 g prawns, defrosted if frozen, slit open, veins removed
and rinsed
seasoned sea salt
5 cloves garlic, crushed
4 T (60 ml) olive oil
1 red chilli, finely sliced, with seeds
freshly ground black pepper
4 T (60 ml) chopped fresh parsley

Season the prawns and leave them in the fridge to firm in a
colander for at least 20 minutes. Preheat the oven to 240 °C.
Toss the prawns with all the remaining ingredients, except half
of the parsley. Place in an ovenproof serving dish and blast roast
in the oven for 10–15 minutes only until they turn pink. Do not
overcook. Sprinkle with remaining parsley and serve straight
away, with fresh country-style bread to mop up the juices.

prawns with garlic and chilli

PEPPERY FETA SPREAD WITH SUN-DRIED TOMATOES

SERVES 8–10

My friend Phill Scott regularly makes this pâté and always gets rave reviews. She is a botanical painter, gardener and potter who has some of the most beautiful serving platters. Her food always looks better than mine!

1 x 225 g tub feta cheese, drained
8 sun-dried tomato quarters
4 T (60 ml) olive oil
1 red chilli, finely sliced, with seeds
1 t (5 ml) freshly ground black pepper
1 x 250 g tub smooth cottage cheese

Place all the ingredients in a processor and process until smooth. Serve at room temperature with fresh pita bread, crostini or crackers.

COOK'S TIP
This recipe can be made a few days in advance and kept in the fridge. Do not freeze.

CITRUS-MARINATED OLIVES WITH CORIANDER

SERVES 6

By marinating the olives their flavour is greatly enhanced. We served this to a group of American visitors and they just loved the fresh citrus taste.

1 x 410 g tin green olives
2 T (30 ml) coriander seeds, crushed
1 lemon, cut into thin slices
1 T (15 ml) grated orange rind
4 cloves garlic, cut into long, thin strips
1 fresh red chilli, finely sliced, with seeds
1 T (15 ml) fresh lemon thyme or 1 t (5 ml) dried thyme
4 T (60 ml) lemon juice
½ cup (125 ml) olive oil
½ bunch fresh coriander, well washed

Place the olives in a sterilised glass jar and add the coriander seeds, lemon slices, orange rind, garlic, chilli and thyme. Shake the lemon juice with the oil and pour over the olives. Leave to marinate for at least a day or up to 2 weeks in the fridge.

Add fresh coriander sprigs just before serving. Serve at room temperature with crusty bread and a soft, young cheese such as goats' cheese or ricotta.

VARIATION
Use a mixture of green and black Calamata olives.

COOK'S TIP
To sterilise the glass jar quickly, half fill with water and microwave for 3 minutes on high (100 per cent). Alternatively, rinse with boiling water or soak in Milton's sterilising fluid.

ROASTED ONION SALAD

SERVES 6

This is trendy and dead easy to make.
Roasting develops and intensifies the flavour of onion,
while smoothing out any harsh notes.

6 large, preferably red, onions
½ cup (125 ml) olive oil
1 T (15 ml) sugar
seasoned sea salt
1 cup (250 ml) watercress
1 cup (250 ml) rocket or baby spinach
200 g block of Parmesan or pecorino cheese
lite Greek dressing

Preheat the oven to 250 °C. Don't peel the onions. Top and tail them and slice each across into 4 thick slices. Spread them out on an oiled baking sheet and brush them with the olive oil. Sprinkle lightly with a little sugar. Season with seasoned sea salt. Bake for about 30 minutes until dark brown and soft. Leave to cool. Discard the outer rings with the skin on.

To serve, divide the greens between 6 medium-sized plates. Top with the roasted onion. Add shavings of Parmesan or pecorino cheese (use a potato peeler) and freshly ground black pepper. Dress with salad dressing and serve.

INDIVIDUAL EGG AND BLUE CHEESE SALADS

SERVES 8–10

This economical starter never fails to please. If you have a
guest who has an aversion to blue cheese, use a well-ripened
Brie or feta cheese instead.

EGG AND BLUE CHEESE MIXTURE
6 hard-boiled eggs
1 x 250 g tub smooth cottage cheese
125 g creamy blue cheese
1 small bunch spring onions with green tops, finely sliced
freshly ground black pepper

4-6 heads of chicory
1 cup (250 ml) rocket, baby spinach or watercress
lite French dressing

French bread

Process all the ingredients for the egg and blue cheese mixture together in a food processor. Smooth the mixture into small individual pâté dishes, then place them on medium-sized plates. Arrange the dressed salad leaves on the side. Serve with oven-crisped rounds of French bread on the side.

Oven crisp the French bread as follows: Preheat the oven to 200 °C. Slice the bread on the diagonal into 1 cm thick slices, brush lightly on both sides with olive oil and arrange on a baking sheet. Dust with garlic and herb seasoning and bake for about 10–12 minutes until golden.

UPSIDE-DOWN CARAMELISED TOMATO AND ONION TART

SERVES 6–8

Make this for a special buffet table. Do the work in stages to simplify preparation. Make the pastry and roast the vegetables the day before. After that it is plain sailing and absolutely worth the effort. This tart looks as good as it tastes.

6–8 very ripe red tomatoes, cut into quarters
herb salad dressing
2 red peppers, seeded and cut into eighths
5 medium-sized onions, sliced in half circles
3 T (45 ml) butter or olive oil
garlic and herb seasoning
¾ cup (150 g) granulated sugar
1 T (15 ml) water
shortcrust pastry (see recipe below)
fresh herbs for garnishing

Preheat the oven to 220 °C. Toss the tomatoes with the dressing and arrange skin-side down in a non-stick roasting pan lined with baking paper. Toss the peppers in a little more dressing and add to the tomatoes. Roast for 35–45 minutes, until nicely browned. Remove from the oven and leave to cool. Turn the oven down to 200 °C.

Sauté the onions in the butter or olive oil, then turn the heat right down. Cover the onions with greaseproof paper as well as a lid. Cook for 20–25 minutes until the onions are soft and mushy. Season. Leave to cool.

In a heavybased saucepan melt and caramelise the sugar over high heat, while shaking the pot all the time – do not stir. Add the tablespoon of water (be careful when adding water as it might spit) to thin the syrup out a little and pour it into a 25 cm ovenproof porcelain flan dish. Tilt the dish to coat the bottom and halfway up the sides. Arrange the cooked tomatoes (skin side down) and the peppers to cover the base of the dish in a pretty pattern. Spoon the onions over the top and smooth.

Cover the top of the pie with shortcrust pastry, making sure it is properly sealed. Trim pastry level with the edge of the dish. Bake at 200 °C for 25–30 minutes until the pastry is crisp and golden brown. Remove from the oven and leave to stand for about 10 minutes. Turn a large round plate upside down on top of the flan dish and invert the pie on the plate. Garnish with fresh herbs, such as basil.

SHORTCRUST PASTRY
1 cup (120 g) cake flour
½ t (2.5 ml) salt
4 T (60 g) butter, fridge temperature
1 egg yolk
2 T (30 ml) cold water

Sift the flour and salt twice and rub in the butter to form coarse crumbs. Mix the egg yolk with cold water and add to the flour. Cut the liquid in with a small knife to form a lumpy mixture. Use your hands to gather and knead the mixture together until it forms a ball. Don't add more water, simply keep working the dough lightly.

Wrap the dough in clingfilm and leave to rest in the fridge (in cooler weather, it is best to leave out of the fridge, as it can become too hard and brittle). Roll out to 1 cm thickness. Fold into thirds and roll out again to 2 mm thickness on a well-floured surface, using a floured rolling pin. (This preliminary rolling makes the dough much easier to handle.)

COOK'S TIP
This pastry freezes well.

upside-down caramelised tomato and onion tart

BAKED PEPPERS WITH CHERRY TOMATOES

SERVES 8

*A beautiful dish with delicious summer flavours
for a buffet table or braai spread.*

2 red peppers, halved lengthways
2 yellow peppers, halved lengthways
olive oil, for brushing
225 g red cherry tomatoes, halved
225 g yellow cherry tomatoes, halved
4 T (60 ml) olive oil
1 T (15 ml) Balsamic vinegar
1–2 t (5–10 ml) honey
4 cloves garlic, finely sliced lengthways
salt and freshly ground black pepper
2 t (10 ml) chopped fresh rosemary
2 t (10 ml) chopped fresh thyme
1 t (5 ml) grated lemon rind

Preheat the oven to 220 °C. Scoop out and discard the seeds from the peppers (leave the stalks for decoration) and place cut side up in a roasting pan. Brush all over with olive oil and roast on the top shelf for 30 minutes. Meanwhile, in a large bowl, toss together the cherry tomatoes, olive oil, vinegar, honey, garlic slivers and seasoning.

Remove the peppers from the oven and spoon in the tomato mixture in equal portions, to fill the pepper halves. Return to the oven and roast for a further 20 minutes until golden and tender. Sprinkle with a mixture of chopped fresh herbs and lemon rind. Glaze with a little extra olive oil. Serve at room temperature with plenty of crusty bread.

VARIATIONS
- Use courgettes in place of yellow cherry tomatoes.
- Use basil in place of rosemary and thyme.

CHICKEN AND PASTA SALAD WITH APPLES AND NUTS

SERVES 6–8

1 cup (250 ml) chicken stock
1 T (15 ml) fresh tarragon or basil, or 1 t (5 ml) dried
2 t (10 ml) medium-strength curry powder
garlic and herb seasoning
6–8 chicken breasts
5 sticks celery, very thinly sliced diagonally
1 bunch spring onions, very thinly sliced diagonally
2 red apples, cored and cut into thin slices
2 cups (500 ml) cooked screw noodles
1 cup (250 ml) honey mustard salad dressing
green salad leaves
1 cup (100 g) coarsely chopped pecan nuts

Heat the chicken stock, herbs and curry to boiling point in a large, heavybased frying pan with a lid. Season the chicken with the garlic and herb seasoning.

Place the chicken breasts in the stock and reduce the heat. Cover the frying pan and simmer slowly for 5–6 minutes. Remove the pan from the heat and allow the chicken to cool to room temperature in the liquid.

Meanwhile, mix the celery lightly with the spring onions and apples. Cut the chicken into strips 1 cm thick, across the grain. Return the chicken to the stock and allow it to stand for 5 minutes to absorb the stock. Mix the chicken and the pasta lightly with the honey mustard salad dressing. Fold in the celery, apples and spring onions.

Line individual plates with lettuce and stack the chicken in the centre. Sprinkle with nuts.

Serve with moist butternut health bread (page 119) or crusty home-made bread and butter.

ITALIAN ANTIPASTO SELECTION

ROAST CAPSICUM SALAD

SERVES 4–5

4 red or yellow peppers
3–4 T (45–60 ml) extra virgin olive oil
1 ripe tomato, peeled, seeded and finely chopped
1 clove garlic, finely chopped
basil leaves, torn into strips
salt and pepper

Roast the peppers in a hot oven, under a grill or over a flame until black and blistered. Place them in a plastic bag to sweat, then peel off the skin and remove the stalk and seeds. Cut the peppers into strips. Retain any juices.

Combine juices with the olive oil, tomato, garlic and basil leaves. Add salt and pepper and combine with the pepper strips. Serve at room temperature.

CROSTINI WITH CHICKEN LIVERS

SERVES 6

500 g chicken livers
3 T (45 ml) butter
3 T (45 ml) olive oil
3 T (45 ml) chopped onion
a few sage leaves
1 T (15 ml) capers
6 thick slices sourdough or Italian casalinga bread

Clean and trim the chicken livers and cut into small pieces. Heat the butter and olive oil in a pan and fry the chopped onion until golden and translucent. Add the sage leaves, capers and livers. Sauté over a medium heat for 5 minutes until lightly browned. Meanwhile, toast the bread under the grill to make the crostini. Roughly mix the livers together with a fork into a coarse, lumpy paste. Season and spread thickly on the crostini. Pop the slices into a warm oven for a minute, then serve.

marinated red roman in vine leaves

'Love is a delightful interval between meeting a beautiful girl and discovering that she looks like a haddock.'

John Barrymore

FISH

MARINATED RED ROMAN
IN VINE LEAVES

SERVES 6

The vine leaves are important for presentation. Nobody likes to look a dead fish in the eye! The ready made sauce makes the preparation of this simple yet delicious dish effortless.

3 red romans (each approximately 25 cm long)
1–2 packets Marinate-in-a-Bag, lemon and herb, or green
peppercorn flavour
seasoned sea salt
12–18 fresh vine leaves
kitchen string
4 T (60 ml) olive oil
½ cup (125 ml) cream

Ask your fishmonger to clean and scale the fish and to remove the backbone but leave the head and tail intact. Slash 3 deep cuts into both fleshy sides. Season inside and out. Marinate the fish in the Marinate-in-a-Bag for 30 minutes.

Remove the fish from the bags and reserve the marinade. Wrap each head in 2–3 vine leaves and secure with string. Cover heads and tails with foil before braaiing.

Heat the oil in a large frying pan, place the fish in the pan and cook for about 5 minutes on each side, or cook on the braai in a hinged clamp grid, also for about 5 minutes on each side.

To make a sauce, bring the remaining marinade to the boil, add the cream and boil for 1 minute.

Serve with a potato salad spiked with chives, and garlic bread.

COOK'S TIP
Late in the season vine leaves tend to be hard. To soften them, soak them in boiling water for 3 minutes, then rinse them under cold water.

VARIATION
Use spinach leaves (blanched) in place of vine leaves.

CAPE SALMON
WITH SMOKED CHEESE SAUCE

SERVES 4

This rich, smooth creamy cheese and mushroom sauce with its gentle, smokey flavour complements fish to perfection.

600 g Cape salmon, filleted and skinned
seasoned sea salt
3 T (45 ml) flour
250 g button mushrooms, sliced
3 T (45 ml) butter
2 T (30 ml) flour
1¼ cups (310 ml) full cream milk
100 g smoked cheese, cubed

Preheat the oven to 220 °C. Season and dust the fish with flour and lay it in a buttered ovenproof dish. Sauté the mushrooms briefly in the butter, add the flour and stir-fry for 1–2 minutes. Add all the milk at once and stir continuously to make a medium-thick sauce. Add the cheese and continue stirring over a very low heat until the cheese is integrated into the sauce. Taste for seasoning. Bake the fish without the sauce for 10 minutes. Then pour the sauce over and continue baking for another 7 minutes.

This is delicious served with parsley potatoes, peas, and a rocket or watercress salad dressed with a lite French dressing.

VARIATION
Use kabeljou or kingklip instead of Cape salmon.

COOK'S TIP
To firm fish and keep it fresh, salt the fresh fish lightly with seasoned sea salt. Do not salt it again during cooking. Place fish in a glass dish and cover with clingfilm or seal in a plastic bag. Place ice packs or plastic bags filled with ice cubes on top of the fish. These will keep it slightly colder than fridge temperature. Return the fish to the fridge, where it will keep for 1 or 2 days.

MALAY SPICED FISH ON A BED OF BUTTERNUT

SERVES 6–8

This is a superb combination of Cape flavours. Serve the fish with rice pilaf decorated with saffron eggs and add colour with a selection of sambal salads. For convenience this dish can be prepared, and baked just before serving.

1.5 kg kabeljou or Cape salmon filleted,
skinned and cut into portions
seasoned sea salt
4 T (60 ml) butter
1 medium butternut, peeled, seeded and
coarsely grated
seasoned sea salt to taste
2 T (30 ml) flour
2 t (10 ml) medium-strength curry
powder or fish masala
pinch cayenne pepper
4 T (60 ml) melted butter
2 cloves garlic, crushed
2 T (30 ml) sun-dried tomato pesto or tomato paste
fresh coriander leaves to garnish

Preheat the oven to 220 °C if you are planning to serve the fish straight after preparing it. Season the fish, cover and chill in the refrigerator.

In a large frying pan, melt the butter until it begins to brown. Add the grated butternut and stir-fry for 5 minutes. Season and spoon into a large ovenproof serving dish. Dust the fish lightly with a mixture of flour, curry powder and cayenne pepper. Lay on the bed of butternut. Brush the fish with a mixture of melted butter, crushed garlic and tomato pesto. It may be prepared to this stage, then covered and refrigerated.

Before serving, bake the fish at 220 °C for 20–25 minutes, depending on the thickness of the fish.

Garnish with fresh coriander.

RICE PILAF

½ cup (125 ml) brown lentils
1 medium onion, chopped
2 T (30 ml) oil
1 T (15 ml) fresh ginger, finely grated
4 cloves garlic, crushed
1 T (15 ml) curry powder
3 cups (750 ml) raw rice
6 cups (1.5 litres) vegetable or chicken stock
garlic and herb seasoning to taste
4 T (60 ml) chopped fresh coriander leaves, or parsley if
coriander is not available

Pour boiling water over the lentils and leave to soak for 1 hour. In a saucepan, sauté the onion in the oil until soft. Add the ginger, garlic and curry powder and stir-fry for 30 seconds. Add the rice, stir through and when well coated with spices and oil, add the stock and well-drained lentils. Boil, with a lid on, for 15 minutes. Taste for seasoning and sprinkle over the chopped coriander or parsley leaves. This pilaf reheats very successfully in the microwave.

SAFFRON EGGS

4–6 small or medium eggs
pinch saffron or turmeric
4 T (60 ml) hot chicken stock

Hard boil the eggs, then peel and slice them in half lengthways. Add the saffron to the boiling hot stock and leave it to draw for 5 minutes until it is bright yellow. Spoon this over the yolks to tint them a deep yellow colour.

SAMBAL SALADS

Sambals such as grated cucumber, finely diced green pepper, finely sliced spring onion, cubed tomato and grated carrot make excellent accompaniments to the spiced fish.

FISH BAKE WITH LEEKS AND BABY PEAS

SERVES 4

The gentle flavours in this dish blend perfectly.

6 small leeks, well washed and trimmed
3 T (45 ml) butter
600–800 g firm white fish (hake, kabeljou or steenbras),
filleted and skinned
seasoned sea salt
flour
1½ cups (375 ml) frozen baby peas (petits pois)
salt
white pepper
pinch sugar
½ cup (125 ml) fresh parsley, chopped

Preheat the oven to 220 °C.

In a saucepan, sweat the leeks slowly in the butter under a blanket of greaseproof paper until soft (about 15 minutes). Meanwhile, season the fish, dust it with a little flour and lay the fillets in a well-buttered ovenproof dish. Toss the frozen peas with the cooked leeks and season to taste with salt, pepper and a pinch of sugar. Spread the vegetables in a layer over the fish fillets. Bake for 20 minutes.

To serve, sprinkle generously with the chopped parsley and serve with chips and a well-dressed tossed salad.

VARIATION

Finely sliced sweet potatoes or beetroot make delicious chips. Cook them separately over moderate heat. Watch that the oil temperature doesn't go higher than 180 °C in a deep fryer.

CURED CAPE SALMON KEBABS WITH HERBED TOMATO SAMBAL

SERVES 4

This is the ideal fish dish to prepare in advance.

600 g Cape salmon, filleted and skinned
2 T (30 ml) brandy or lemon juice
2 t (10 ml) seasoned sea salt
1 T (15 ml) sugar
chopped fresh herbs (fennel or dill)
satay sticks
olive oil

To cure the fish, brush it with brandy or lemon juice and season it with seasoned sea salt and sugar. Sprinkle with herbs and leave it covered with clingfilm in the coldest part of the fridge overnight or for 6 hours with an ice brick on top. Cut the cured fish into cubes and thread onto skewers. Brush with oil and grill slowly until just done.

Serve with herbed tomato sambal, fresh olive bread and a green salad.

HERBED TOMATO SAMBAL

4 large ripe tomatoes, diced
3 cloves garlic, crushed
½ cup (125 ml) chopped fresh basil or origanum
½ cup (125 ml) fresh coriander leaves
2 T (30 ml) Balsamic vinegar or lemon juice
grated rind of 1 lemon
3 T (45 ml) finely sliced chives
1–2 hot chillies, finely sliced
4 T (60 ml) olive oil

Combine all the ingredients and serve immediately. Tomato sambal should be freshly made, otherwise the tomato wilts.

cured cape salmon kebabs with herbed tomato sambal

BLACKENED FISH
WITH AUBERGINE AND RED PEPPERS

SERVES 6

This is one of our favourites for summer entertaining alfresco.
Serve it at room temperature if you are preparing in advance.
Calculate 200 g of fish per person.

CREOLE SPICE MIX
1½ t (7.5 ml) cayenne pepper
1 T (15 ml) paprika
1½ t (7.5 ml) freshly ground black pepper
1 chilli, finely sliced, with seeds
5 cloves garlic, crushed
5 T (75 ml) sunflower or Canola oil

6–8 kingklip, kabeljou or Cape salmon loin
portions of equal thickness
seasoned sea salt
3 medium to large aubergines, cut into thick rounds
seasoned sea salt
3–4 red peppers, seeded and cut into eighths
olive oil

baked fish with olive topping

Mix all the ingredients for the Creole spice mix to form a paste. Season the fish and brush all over with the spice mix. Cover and refrigerate until just before cooking.

Salt the aubergines and leave them to stand in a colander for at least 30 minutes. Preheat the oven to 220 °C. Rinse the aubergines and pat very dry. Toss together with the pepper strips in olive oil. Spread the vegetables out in a single layer on a greaseproof, lined baking sheet (saves washing up). Bake for 40 minutes, until nicely browned. They may be cooked in advance and reheated in the microwave if you prefer to serve the dish hot.

Before serving, grill the fish until it is just done (see Cook's tips below). Place a portion of fish on a slice of aubergine and top with the peppers. Garnish with fresh herbs.

VEGETARIAN VARIATION
Top the roasted aubergine slices with thick rounds of mozzarella cheese, and flash under the grill to brown. Top with roasted peppers and sun-dried tomato quarters and serve.

COOK'S TIPS
■ Nothing overcooks more easily than fish, so keeping a close eye on it is crucial. When the flesh becomes whitish, test it with a fork – it should be just beginning to flake. If it starts drawing water, you are overcooking the fish and it will be dry.
■ To calculate the cooking time, measure the thickest part of the fish with a ruler placed upright next to the fillet or whole fish. Calculate 7–10 minutes at 200 °C for every 1 cm.

BAKED FISH WITH OLIVE TOPPING

The robust Mediterranean flavour of this topping is outstanding on fish. For convenience I have used anchovies in oil, but a far superior option is salt-cured anchovies bought from Italian delicatessens. They come in barrels and you can buy what you need.

800 g firm white fish (Cape salmon, kabeljou, steenbras or kingklip), filleted and skinned
seasoned sea salt
flour
olive oil

TOPPING
½ cup (125 ml) sun-dried tomato quarters in olive oil vinaigrette, drained
4 T (60 ml) stoned black calamata olives
¼ cup (60 ml) basil leaves, or fresh origanum or parsley when basil is out of season
1 T (15 ml) green peppercorns, drained from brine
3 cloves garlic
1 x 50 g tin anchovy fillets in oil (use the oil as well)
2 T (30 ml) capers
3 T (45 ml) olive oil
freshly ground black pepper

Preheat the oven to 220 °C. Season the fish, dust with flour and lay in an ovenproof dish. Brush each fillet with olive oil.

Briefly chop all the ingredients for the topping together in a processor or with a cook's knife to form a rough-textured paste. Spread on top of the fish. Bake for 20 minutes.

Serve with baked polenta and peppers.

VARIATION
Pan-fry the fish and spread topping over once cooked.

GRILLED MARINATED TUNNY

This superb dish is always part of our summer holiday fish buffet.

1–1.5 kg piece of tuna or yellowtail or Cape salmon fillets, cut into 1–1.5 cm thick slices
seasoned sea salt
olive oil

HERB AND OLIVE SAUCE
¾ cup (180 ml) chopped flat-leaf parsley
¾ cup (180 ml) whole fresh basil or marjoram leaves
4–6 cloves garlic, peeled and sliced lengthways into thin strips
1 cup (250 ml) extra virgin olive oil
1 t (5 ml) Balsamic vinegar
1 T (15 ml) lemon juice

Salt the fish lightly, brush with olive oil and place on a very hot grill or griddle pan, pushing it flat with a lifter. Turn once it is marked and brown, and cook the other side. Do not overcook the fish; it must still be soft on the inside. As it stands it will continue cooking.

Stir all the ingredients for the herb and olive sauce together. Keep at room temperature. Spoon over the cooked fish and leave to cool. Serve at room temperature. This is excellent with a green salad and a tomato-mozzarella salad.

COOK'S TIP
Do not chop the basil or marjoram leaves or they will turn black. Leave them whole or tear them by hand.

SMOKED FISH AND MUSHROOM PIE WITH BUTTERNUT TOPPING

SERVES 8

This is one of those recipes that takes time and generates a lot of washing up, but it is well worth it. It could be made a day in advance and baked just before serving.

600 g smoked haddock
½ cup (125 ml) vegetable stock
250 g smoked mussels
1 cup (250 ml) milk
½ cup (125 ml) cream
1 onion, sliced
1 large carrot, scraped and sliced
1 small bay leaf
sprig lemon thyme or pinch dried thyme
3 T (45 ml) butter, softened
2 T (30 ml) flour
250 g sliced button mushrooms
4 hard-boiled eggs, rubbed through a coarse sieve
2 T (30 ml) finely chopped parsley
seasoned sea salt

TOPPING
4 potatoes, cubed
1½ cups (375 ml) cubed butternut
½ cup (125 ml) warm milk
1 T (15 ml) butter
seasoned sea salt

Poach the haddock in the vegetable stock for 5 minutes in a heavybased frying pan covered with both greaseproof paper and a lid. Remove from the heat and leave to stand, covered, for another 5 minutes. Reserve the liquid. Skin and flake the fish and add the flaked fish to the mussels.

Warm the milk, add the reserved stock as well as the cream, onion, carrot, bay leaf and thyme. As soon as the mixture comes to the boil, draw the saucepan to one side and leave the vegetables to draw for 20–30 minutes.

Mix the butter and flour to a smooth paste. Strain the vegetables, retaining the stock, and thicken the stock with the butter-flour mixture. Cook for 3 minutes while stirring continuously. Add the mushrooms, eggs and parsley. Taste for seasoning. Add the flaked fish mixture and spoon it into a buttered ovenproof dish.

Preheat the oven to 200 °C.

To make the topping, steam the potatoes and butternut until soft, then put them through a potato ricer or mash by hand with a potato masher. Add the warm milk and butter and season to taste. Spoon the potato and butternut mixture over the fish. Bake until it is warmed through and lightly browned (about 20–25 minutes). Serve with green vegetables or a salad.

VARIATION
Kosher households can replace the mussels
with peppered mackerel.

PEPPERED MUSSELS

SERVES 4

*There can surely be no better or simpler method to
prepare fresh mussels.*

**1 kg fresh black mussels in closed shells
freshly ground black pepper
chopped parsley**

Remove the beards from the mussels and place them in a large
frying pan or saucepan. Cover with a tight-fitting lid and place
over a high heat. Shake the pan and cook until the mussels
open. Remove the lid and grind a generous amount of black
pepper over the mussels. The mussels will give off their own
delicious liquid while cooking. Add a handful of chopped parsley
and serve immediately with some good bread to mop up the
juices and a well-dressed green salad with onion rings. Provide
finger bowls with a slice of lemon.

Purists believe metal spoils the fresh flavour of mussels, so
demonstrate to your guests how to eat the mussels by picking
out the flesh with a pair of mussel shells as pincers, instead of
knives and forks.

COOK'S TIP

Cultivated mussels grown on ropes are clean of sand and
there is no need to soak them in cold water first, or to strain
the mussel liquid after cooking. Mussels picked off the rocks,
on the other hand, can be sandy and must be presoaked in
clean water for 1 hour, and the cooking juices strained.

LEMON FISH IN CREAM SAUCE

SERVES 6

This recipe is great if you're in a hurry. It's always a winner.

**1.5 kg firm white fish (kabeljou or kingklip),
filleted and skinned
seasoned sea salt
1 Marinate-in-a-Bag, lemon and herb flavour, or lemon and
herb Coat & Cook sauce
1 cup (250 ml) cream
½ cup (125 ml) freshly grated Parmesan
fresh herbs to garnish**

Preheat the oven to 220 °C. Cut the fish into neat portions and
season. Place in the marinade or sauce and leave to stand for
20 minutes at room temperature. Remove the fish from the
marinade and place in a single layer in a buttered ovenproof
dish. Add the cream to the remaining marinade and shake or stir
to mix. Pour the sauce over the fish and sprinkle the Parmesan
on top. Bake uncovered for 20 minutes.

Garnish with freshly chopped herbs, such as basil, origanum
or parsley, and serve with buttered tagliatelle noodles.

baby chickens with pear, bacon and pecan nut stuffing

'No matter how happily

a woman may be married,

it always pleases her to discover

there is a nice man

who wishes she were not.'

H.L. Mencken

POULTRY

BABY CHICKENS WITH PEAR, BACON AND PECAN NUT STUFFING

SERVES 4

Prepared in this way, one baby chicken easily serves two people. Served with oven-roasted vegetables, it has a healthy, contemporary appeal.

2 baby chickens
seasoned sea salt
2 T (30 ml) butter
1 onion, diced
6 rashers bacon, diced
½ cup (50 g) pecan nuts, roughly chopped
2 T (30 ml) finely chopped fresh sage
or 2 t (10 ml) dried sage
1 clove garlic, crushed
2 pears, diced
2 T (30 ml) chopped parsley
⅔ cup (160 ml) soft breadcrumbs
2 t (10 ml) grated fresh lemon rind
1 x 200 ml lemon and herb Coat & Cook sauce, or ½ cup
(125 ml) olive oil and 4 T (60 ml) fresh lemon juice

Preheat the oven to 190 °C. Rinse and pat the baby chickens dry. Season inside and out. Set aside.

Melt the butter in a saucepan, then add the onion and bacon and cook until soft. Add the nuts, sage, garlic, pears and parsley. Cook for a further 2 minutes. Mix in the breadcrumbs and lemon rind. Stuff the baby chickens with this mixture and tie the legs together with string. Place in a smallish ovenproof dish and pour over the sauce or olive oil and lemon juice mixture. Bake uncovered for 50 minutes, until golden. Serve with oven-roasted seasonal vegetables (see recipe on page 42).

CHICKEN THIGHS WITH RED PEPPERS AND SUN-DRIED TOMATOES

SERVES 4–5

Casserole cooking at its best. A one-dish main course that should be served with rice, polenta or Italian bread and a well-dressed green salad.

3 T (45 ml) olive or Canola oil
8 chicken thighs
2 t (10 ml) garlic and herb seasoning
12 fat cloves garlic, cut in half lengthways
½ cup (125 ml) dry white wine
½ cup (125 ml) chicken stock
½ cup (125 ml) lemon and herb Coat & Cook sauce
3 red peppers, seeded and sliced into quarters
1 red chilli, sliced, with seeds
½ packet (about 120 ml) sun-dried tomato quarters, drained
½ cup (125 ml) stoned black Calamata olives
freshly ground black pepper
fresh herbs (basil, origanum or parsley)

Heat the oil in a heavybased saucepan and brown the chicken pieces all over to crisp the skin and cook the surplus fat out of the skin. Remove the chicken with a slotted spoon and set aside on a plate. Season it with garlic and herb seasoning.

Pour out the remaining fat from the saucepan. Briefly toss the garlic in the pan browning, then add the wine and boil fast to reduce by half. Add the stock and bring back to the boil. Place the chicken in the liquid. Pour the lemon and herb sauce over the chicken and cover with a tight-fitting lid. Turn the heat right down and simmer for 30 minutes.

Add the peppers, chilli, sun-dried tomatoes and olives. Continue simmering for another 30 minutes.

Thicken the sauce with a little potato flour or cornflour. Taste for seasoning and add freshly ground black pepper and herbs.

CHICKEN STIR-FRY
WITH NOODLES AND VEGETABLES

SERVES 4

A quick, easy and healthy dish, just right for today's lifestyle.

2 cups (500 ml) capelli d'angelo
(angelhair pasta) or tagliatelli
6 skinless chicken breasts, thinly sliced across the grain
1 x Marinate-in-a-Bag, honey and soy flavour
2–3 T (30–45 ml) sesame or sunflower oil
1 cup (250 ml) button mushrooms, sliced
1 red pepper, sliced into strips
1 chilli, finely sliced, with seeds
1 bunch spring onions with green tops, finely sliced

Cook the pasta in boiling, salted water until *al dente*. Drain well when cooked.

Meanwhile, place the sliced chicken in the bag and massage well for 1–2 minutes. Leave it in the bag at room temperature for up to 30 minutes.

Remove the chicken from the marinade and stir-fry in the oil over very high heat until just done. Add the vegetables, pasta and remaining marinade. Stir-fry until heated through.

Serve with a selection of salad sambals, such as diced cucumber and whole cherry tomatoes.

VARIATION
Use chicken thighs in place of guinea fowl in the following recipe for Guinea Fowl Casserole with Red Wine, and reduce the cooking time to 45 minutes.

GUINEA FOWL CASSEROLE
WITH RED WINE

SERVES 4

A long, slow, moist cooking method is the best way to tenderise guinea fowl and to develop the flavour.

2 large guinea fowl, cut into portions
2 T (30 ml) red wine vinegar
seasoned sea salt
flour
4 T (60 ml) olive oil
3 sticks celery, chopped
3 cloves garlic, sliced
2 T (30 ml) tomato pesto or tomato paste
4 fresh ripe tomatoes, skinned and chopped
¾ cup (180 ml) red wine
salt and freshly ground black pepper
½ cup (125 ml) water
½ cup (125 ml) stoned green olives
½ cup (125 ml) seedless raisins, briefly rinsed
with boiling water
2 T (30 ml) chopped fresh parsley
fresh lemon juice, if desired

Rub the guinea fowl pieces all over with the vinegar, cover and leave for a few hours at room temperature.

Drain, season and dust with flour. Heat the olive oil in a heavybased saucepan and brown the pieces briskly. Remove with a slotted spoon and set aside. Add the celery, garlic, tomato pesto, fresh tomato, red wine, seasoning and water to the saucepan and boil briskly to reduce. Add the browned meat. Bring to a simmer, cover with greaseproof paper and a lid and simmer very gently for 1½ hours, until the guinea fowl is tender. Add the remaining ingredients and cook, uncovered, for a further 10 minutes. Taste for seasoning. It may need a squeeze of fresh lemon juice and a pinch of sugar.

SUMMER CHICKEN
MARINATED IN GARLIC AND HERBS

SERVES 6

*This is a supurb recipe – one of my favourites –
and outstanding for preparing in advance. It is ideal
to serve on a cold buffet table, it is economical and it
always gets rave reviews.*

1 large free-range chicken
2 large carrots, sliced thickly
1 large onion, quartered
6 cloves garlic, peeled and finely sliced
8 t (40 ml) chicken stock powder
4 cups (1 litre) boiling water

MARINADE
1 cup (250 ml) extra virgin olive oil
½ cup (125 ml) fresh origanum, basil or sage leaves
10 cloves garlic, sliced into fine strips
1 t (5 ml) salt
freshly ground black pepper

**2 cups (500 ml) chicken stock, reserved from
cooked chicken**

Skin the chicken by simply pulling the skin off the body and
thighs. Don't bother with the wings. Place it breast up in a heavybased saucepan with the carrots, onion and garlic. Dissolve the
stock powder in the boiling water and pour it over the chicken.
Cover with greaseproof paper and then a tight-fitting lid. Simmer
slowly for 1½ hours until the chicken is very tender and starts to
come away from the bone.

Mix the marinade ingredients together and leave to stand at
room temperature to allow the flavours to develop.

Remove the chicken from the stove and turn it over, breast
down. Leave it to cool slowly in the poaching liquid. When cool,
remove the chicken and reserve 2 cups (500 ml) of the stock for
the sauce (keep the rest of the stock for soup or another recipe).
Remove the onion and carrot.

Strip the meat from the bone into long, thin strips. Beat the
reserved stock into the marinade. Layer the chicken and sauce
in a porcelain dish and cover with clingfilm, pushing the clingfilm
down onto the mixture to expel as much air as possible.
Refrigerate for a few hours or overnight, to let the flavours
mature. Bring to room temperature before serving.

Serve with a well-dressed green salad and some Italian
country-style bread to mop up the delicious sauce.

CHICKEN KEBABS
WITH MINT VINAIGRETTE

SERVES 4

An unusual and refreshing combination, ideal for summer.

6 skinless chicken breast fillets
1½ t (7.5 ml) curry powder
2 t (10 ml) seasoned sea salt
½ t (2.5 ml) ground cumin
6-8 satay sticks

MINT VINAIGRETTE
4 T (60 ml) lemon juice
4 T (60 ml) finely chopped fresh mint leaves
½ t (2.5 ml) ground coriander
½ cup (125 ml) Canola or sunflower oil
2 T (30 ml) good quality soy sauce
salt and pepper to taste

Cut the breasts into 3 cm cubes. Mix the seasonings together
and toss cubes in this to coat them. Skewer each kebab with two
satay sticks. It simplifies turning.

Mix all the ingredients for the vinaigrette together and
marinate the kebabs for at least 30 minutes. Grill until just done.

summer chicken marinated in garlic and herbs

CHICKEN BREASTS AND ROASTED VEGETABLES ON A BED OF NOODLES

SERVES 6

This is a good way to add interest to chicken breasts.

2 medium aubergines, diced
3 large red peppers, diced
4 T (60 ml) olive oil
300–450 g cooked Chinese long-life noodles
6 chicken breasts, cut into strips across the grain
2 t (10 ml) garlic and herb seasoning
2 T (30 ml) flour
3 T (45 ml) olive or Canola oil
1 cup (250 ml) chicken stock
3 cloves garlic, crushed
1 red chilli, finely sliced, with seeds

Preheat the oven to 220 °C or turn on the grill.

Salt the aubergines and place them in a colander to drain the bitter juices. Rinse. Toss the peppers and aubergines in ¼ cup (62.5 ml) olive oil. Arrange in a single layer in a lined or non-stick swiss roll pan. Roast for 20 minutes until soft and browned or grill until nicely browned.

Prepare the noodles by boiling them in salted water until *al dente*, then draining and tossing them with a knob of butter.

Toss the chicken strips lightly in a mixture of the seasoning and flour. Warm the 3 T (45 ml) oil in a heavybased frying pan and stir-fry the chicken until lightly browned. Add the chicken stock and simmer slowly for 10 minutes.

Add the garlic and chilli, then add the roasted vegetables and reheat to boiling point. Taste for seasoning.

Serve the chicken on a bed of the cooked, buttered noodles.

OVEN-ROASTED SEASONAL VEGETABLES

yellow, red and orange peppers, sliced into strips
carrots, sliced into rings
aubergines, diced, salted, rinsed and drained of juices
beetroot, steamed and diced
mushrooms
baby onions
olive oil
seasoned sea salt

Toss any seasonal vegetables of your choice with a little olive oil and season lightly. Roast for 45 minutes. (Cook the beetroot separately to prevent the colour from bleeding.)

To freshen up the colour after roasting, toss the vegetables with chopped fresh parsley or chives and arrange attractively on a serving platter. They are also delicious sprinkled with crumbled blue cheese.

QUAIL'S EGGS WRAPPED IN CHICKEN

SERVES 4

These little eggs look lovely halved and served as a snack with drinks. Alternatively, use hen's eggs and serve them as a main course with salad. They are particularly good for a picnic.

16 quail's eggs or 8 hen's eggs
½ cup (125 ml) fresh white breadcrumbs
6 uncooked chicken breasts, finely chopped in a food processor or minced
1 T (15 ml) finely chopped fresh parsley
1 t (5 ml) mustard powder
1 t (5 ml) garlic and herb seasoning
flour
extra fresh white breadcrumbs
oil for deep frying

Boil the quail's eggs for 3–4 minutes (or 9 minutes for hen's eggs). Shell them. Mix the breadcrumbs with the finely chopped chicken, parsley, mustard and seasoning. Divide the meat mixture into 16 small meatballs (or 8 for hen's eggs). Press or roll each one flat on a floured work surface until it is large enough to wrap around the egg completely, and sprinkle it lightly with flour. Wrap one egg at a time in the flattened chicken. Wet your hands lightly with cold water and roll the eggs in the chicken layer between your hands to make a neat, round shape. Make sure that there are no breaks in the layer of chicken, or the oil will penetrate the chicken during cooking and the chicken will not adhere to the egg.

Moisten the eggs with a little water and then roll in breadcrumbs, then between your hands again to make sure the crumbs adhere well. Refrigerate for 30 minutes.

Deep fry in moderately hot oil (180 °C in a deep fryer) until golden brown. Do not allow the oil to get too hot, or the chicken layer will not cook through. When cool, halve each egg lengthways, preferably with an electric knife.

QUICK CHICKEN CURRY WITH POTATOES

SERVES 4

This curry is aromatic rather than hot. If you prefer it hotter, add extra chilli.

6 medium potatoes, peeled and cubed
4 T (60 ml) oil
6 chicken breasts
salt and pepper
1 onion, chopped
4 t (20 ml) grated fresh ginger
4 cloves garlic, finely chopped
½–1 red chilli, thinly sliced
2 t (10 ml) turmeric
4 cardamom pods, cut open to release seeds
2 t (10 ml) curry powder
1 t (5 ml) ground cumin
grated rind of 1 lemon
2 t (10 ml) garlic and herb seasoning
1 cup (250 ml) chicken stock
2 T (30 ml) lemon juice
fresh coriander leaves

Cut the chicken breasts into thin strips, across the grain. Heat the oil in a large, deep frying pan, and stir-fry the chicken until just cooked. Remove with a slotted spoon and season with salt and pepper. Add the onion, ginger and garlic to the remaining oil in the pan and sauté slowly until the onion is soft. Add the chilli, turmeric, cardamom, curry powder, cumin and lemon rind. Mix well. Stir-fry for 1 minute. Add the garlic and herb seasoning and potato cubes and mix well. Add the chicken stock and heat to boiling point. Simmer for about 15 minutes until the potatoes are just tender. Add the chicken strips and lemon juice and simmer for 5–10 minutes, then taste for seasoning. Spoon into a serving dish and sprinkle with coriander leaves.

CURRIED BUTTER CHICKEN

SERVES 4–6

*I believe this recipe originated when a restaurant
chef who had some left over chicken curry decided to
perk it up by adding tomato and butter –
a great dish was born.
It's a good dish to prepare in
advance as the flavours improve after a day.*

8 chicken thighs
4 cups (1 litre) chicken stock
juice of 1 lemon
1 T (15 ml) chicken masala or medium curry powder
2 t (10 ml) seasoned sea salt
1 large onion, sliced
1 green pepper, diced
4 T (60 ml) sunflower oil
3 cardamom pods, cut open to release seeds
2 cinnamon sticks
5 cloves garlic, crushed
1 T (15 ml) freshly grated ginger
½ T (7.5 ml) garam masala (see recipe below)
½ T (7.5 ml) turmeric
1 T (15 ml) curry leaves (optional)
2 green chillies, finely sliced with seeds
1 large, ripe tomato
3 T (45 ml) tomato paste
4–6 T (60–90 ml) butter
1 bunch fresh coriander, well washed

Remove the skin and bone from the chicken and cut the meat
into cubes. Discard the skin but add the bones to the chicken
stock. Microwave or simmer the stock to extract all the flavour
from the bones while preparing the rest of the ingredients.

Toss the chicken in lemon juice and then sprinkle and toss
with chicken masala and seasoning. Cover and set aside, at
room temperature.

Sauté the onion and green pepper slowly in the oil until
soft. Add the cardamom seeds, cinnamon sticks, garlic, ginger,
garam masala, turmeric, curry leaves and chilli. Stir-fry for
1–2 minutes to allow all the flavours to develop.

Soak the tomato in boiling water for a few minutes to loosen
the skin, then peel and chop it. Add it with the tomato paste and
about 2 cups (500 ml) of the chicken stock to the ingredients in
the pan. Do not add any of the bones. Simmer for 10 minutes.

Add the cubed chicken and lemon juice and bring to the boil.
Add more stock if necessary. Simmer slowly for about
35 minutes until the chicken is tender. Stir in the butter and taste
for seasoning.

Pull the coriander leaves off the stems and sprinkle on top of
the curry just before serving. Serve with rice and sambals.

GARAM MASALA

*Garam masala is a mixture of ground spices. It is available
from speciality spice shops, but you can make your own.*

4 T (60 ml) coriander seeds
2 T (30 ml) cumin
1 T (15 ml) whole black peppercorns
2 t (5 ml) cardamom pods
4 cinnamon sticks, each measuring 7 cm
1 t (5 ml) whole cloves
1 whole nutmeg, grated

Stir-fry each spice – except for the nutmeg – separately in a
small non-stick pan. As each spice starts to smell fragrant,
remove it from the heat and turn it onto a plate to cool. After
roasting the cardamom, cut open the pods and use the seeds.
Place the roasted spices in an electric blender or coffee grinder
and blend to a fine powder, or grind the spices by hand in a
mortar with a pestle. Add the grated nutmeg. Store in the fridge
in a glass jar with an airtight lid.

CURRY POWDER FOR MEAT AND POULTRY

400 g (100 ml) coriander seeds
150 g (200 ml) aniseed
150 g (200 ml) cumin
150 g (500 ml) dried chillies
30 g (50 ml) ground cinnamon
30 g (50 ml) black peppercorns
2 t (5-10 ml) whole cloves
70 g (120 ml) ground turmeric

Dry-fry each ingredient separately in a non-stick pan, except for the turmeric. Blend the roasted ingredients in a blender or in a mortar and pestle until fine. Mix in the turmeric. Store in an airtight container.

CURRY POWDER FOR FISH AND SEAFOOD

400 g (100 ml) coriander seeds
150 g (200 ml) aniseed
150 g (200 ml) cumin
100 g (165 ml) whole white peppercorns
150 g (500 ml) dried chillies
70 g (120 ml) ground turmeric
50 g (120 ml) cardamom pods
90 g (150 ml) ground fenugreek

Dry-fry all the ingredients separately in a small non-stick pan, except for the turmeric. Blend the roasted ingredients in a blender or mortar and pestle until fine, then mix in the turmeric powder. Store in an airtight container.

curried butter chicken

ultimate leg of lamb with rosemary roast potatoes

'Cooking is like love. It should be

entered into with abandon, or not at all.'

Harriet van Horne

MEAT

ULTIMATE LEG OF LAMB

SERVES 6–8

Marina Searle-Tripp, former food editor of Sarie *and* Femina, *is an old friend and was more than willing to share her delicious recipe for leg of lamb with anchovies.*

1 x 2 kg leg of lamb – do not cut the shank bone
4 cloves garlic, cut into slivers
3 sprigs rosemary snipped into 2 cm lengths
garlic and herb seasoning
1 x 50 g tin flat anchovy fillets in oil
2 T (30 ml) olive oil

Lard the lamb with garlic and rosemary. Mash the anchovies with the anchovy and olive oils to form a rough paste. Season meat with garlic and herb seasoning. Rub the paste into the lamb and refrigerate for a couple of hours or overnight. Bring meat to room temperature before roasting.

Preheat the oven to 220 °C. Place the lamb on a rack in a roasting pan. Add 2 cups of water to the pan and roast the meat for 30 minutes. Reduce the heat to 180 °C and roast for another 1–1½ hours or until cooked to your preference. Baste from time to time with the meat juices in the bottom of the pan.

Remove the lamb from the oven and allow to rest for 10 minutes before carving. Strain the pan juices, remove fat, heat and serve as a sauce. Serve with rosemary roast potatoes.

ROSEMARY ROAST POTATOES
1.5 kg medium-sized potatoes, scrubbed
½ cup (125 ml) olive or canola oil
4 T (60 ml) chopped fresh rosemary or 1 T (15 ml) dried
2 t (10 ml) seasoned sea salt

Cut potatoes into wedges and towel dry. Place in a baking dish and pour oil over. Sprinkle with rosemary, tossing to coat evenly. Season. Bake on the lower shelf of the oven at the same time as the lamb, until brown and crisp.

LAMB SHANKS WITH HERBS AND LEMON

SERVES 6

4–6 lamb shanks, excess fat removed
1 T (15 ml) olive or Canola oil
seasoned sea salt
2 medium onions, sliced into thick rings
3 medium carrots, peeled and chopped
2 sticks celery, chopped
4 cloves garlic, crushed
2 T (30 ml) tomato pesto or paste
4 t (20 ml) garlic and herb seasoning
½ cup (125 ml) lemon juice or white wine
4 cups (1 litre) chicken stock
freshly ground black pepper

GREMOLADA
½ cup (125 ml) chopped parsley
4 cloves garlic, crushed
grated rind of 1 large lemon

Preheat the oven to 180 °C. Heat the oil in a large cast-iron pot over high heat. Brown the meat in the oil in batches. Remove, season well with seasoned sea salt and set aside. Reserve 2 T (30 ml) fat in the pan and drain off the rest.

Add the onions, carrots, celery, garlic, tomato pesto and garlic and herb seasoning. Sauté the vegetables for about 3–4 minutes until they begin to soften. Add the lemon juice or white wine and the stock and stir with a wooden spoon. Bring to the boil. Add the shanks. Cover the pot with a lid and bake in the oven for about 2 hours. Remove the lid and bake for about 30 minutes more until the shanks are brown and meltingly tender.

Carefully remove the pot from the oven. Transfer the meat to a warm serving dish and blot the excess fat from the remaining gravy with a double layer of absorbent kitchen paper. Taste for seasoning and adjust if necessary, then pour the sauce over the meat.

Prepare the gremolada mixture by mixing all the ingredients together. Sprinkle over the meat. Serve with parsley rice, to absorb the sauce.

VARIATION

BRAISED LAMB SHANKS WITH WHITE WINE AND MINT

Add 1 lemon, cut into quarters, to the braising liquid. Add 1 T (15 ml) chopped mint leaves and replace the lemon juice with white wine. Stir in 1 T (15 ml) grated lemon rind and 1 extra tablespoon (15 ml) finely chopped mint leaves to the braising liquid after the fat has been removed. Sprinkle the gremolada over. Serve with garlic-flavoured mashed potato.

LAMB CURRY

SERVES 4–5

This is the ideal dish if you like mild but aromatic curry.

1 kg lamb shank, cut into 3 cm pieces
5 cm piece ginger, peeled and finely grated
1½ t (7.5 ml) seasoned sea salt
110 g butter
2 medium onions, peeled, halved and thinly sliced
1 T (15 ml) coriander seeds
2 t (10 ml) black peppercorns
12 cardamom pods
12 whole cloves
½ cup (100 g) ground almonds
3½ cups (875 ml) boiling water
½ cup (125 ml) cream
2 t (10 ml) turmeric
1½ t (7.5 ml) sugar
3 medium cloves garlic, peeled and thinly sliced
4 small lemons
6 sprigs fresh coriander
1 packet lightly flavoured poppadums

Place the meat on a board and sprinkle well with the ginger and sea salt. Set aside. In a large saucepan sauté the onions in the butter over low heat for 10–15 minutes until soft and transparent, stirring often. Meanwhile, place the coriander seeds, peppercorns, cardamom pods and cloves in a pepper mill and grind into a bowl. Place the ground almonds in a medium-sized dish. Pour the boiling water over. Stir well. Add the cream, turmeric and sugar.

Add the garlic to the onions and sauté for a further 5 minutes. Increase the heat to moderate and add the ground-spice mixture and meat. Fry for 5–7 minutes until the meat browns lightly. Stir constantly. Stir in the almond and cream mixture, bring to boiling point and stir well to coat the meat.

Reduce the heat to very low and simmer, covered with a tight–fitting lid, for about 1 hour 40 minutes until the meat is very tender. Stir now and then to ensure that the gravy doesn't stick to the base of the saucepan. The gravy should resemble thick cream and should cover the meat well. Taste and season. Stir in the juice from 2 of the lemons and transfer the curry to a heated serving dish.

Cut the other 2 lemons into wedges and use as a garnish with fresh coriander sprigs.

Fry the poppadums according to the instructions on the packet and serve with the curry, Basmati rice, green beans, cucumber and onion sambals.

LAMB AND VEAL ROLL WITH PARMESAN

SERVES 6

The contrast between light and dark meat in this dish is visually very striking. It is ideally suited for entertaining as it can be prepared well in advance. The gelatine in the recipe prevents the roll from breaking up when carved. Ask your butcher to leave the long piece of rib-flap in place to make rolling of the loin easier, and reserve the bones to make the gravy.

1 kg loin of lamb, boned (bones reserved)
garlic and herb seasoning
2 T (30 ml) tomato pesto or tomato paste
½ cup (125 ml) Parmesan or pecorino cheese
2 t (10 ml) gelatine
500 g veal fillet, or 2 pork fillets or 4 chicken breasts
2 t (10 ml) seasoned sea salt
2 T (30 ml) flour
olive oil
2 onions, roughly chopped
2 carrots, roughly chopped
2 sticks celery, roughly chopped
2 bay leaves
10 whole peppercorns
3 cups (750 ml) boiling water

GRAVY
½ cup (125 ml) sweet Marsala or muscadel wine, or ruby Port
1–2 t (5–10 ml) potato flour or cornflour
2 T (30 ml) butter or 4 T (60 ml) cream
lemon juice

Preheat the oven to 200 °C. Season the inside of the lamb generously with the garlic and herb seasoning and spread the tomato pesto over the inside. Mix the Parmesan or pecorino cheese with the gelatine and sprinkle this over the inside of the lamb. Place the veal fillet along the length on the underside of the loin. Roll up and tie with string at regular intervals. Season well. Dust the outside of the roll with flour and brush it generously with olive oil.

To roast, place the reserved lamb bones, onions, carrots and celery into a roasting pan. Add the bay leaves, whole peppercorns and boiling water. Place a rack over the pan and position the meat roll on the rack. Roast for 45–50 minutes until medium-rare. Use a meat thermometer for best results – it should register 71 °C.

Lightly cover the meat and leave to rest for 10–15 minutes while making the gravy. Strain the bones and vegetables through a colander into a saucepan. Add the sweet wine and reduce the liquid over a high heat – keep on tasting until the flavour is balanced. Thicken if necessary with a little potato flour or cornflour and beat in the butter or cream. Taste, and if it is too sweet, add a squeeze of lemon juice.

Serve with creamy mashed or crisp roast potatoes, a mixture of seasonal green vegetables and roasted baby beetroot.

TO PREPARE IN ADVANCE
Roast the meat and allow to cool. Carve. Prepare the gravy and reserve it in a sauce boat. Arrange the meat on a heat-resistant platter, spoon a little of the gravy over it, and cover with clingfilm. To serve, preheat the oven to 190 °C. Remove the clingfilm, cover the platter with wet greaseproof paper and reheat for 20 minutes at 190 °C. Reheat the gravy in the microwave.

lamb and veal roll with parmesan

GRANDMA'S POT ROAST BEEF

SERVES 5

We have almost forgotten how good beef tastes when it is simply prepared with the minimum of ingredients to detract from its robust flavour. Red meat in moderation is great stuff! This method is faster than oven roasting and excellent for those who love their roast beef tender and just cooked through.

1 kg well-ripened topside, silverside, rib-eye or sirloin
salt and pepper
4 T (60 ml) olive oil
1 bay leaf
12 fat cloves garlic

Place the meat in a medium-sized, oval-shaped, heavy cast-iron saucepan. Season well and rub it all over with the olive oil. Add the bay leaf and garlic. Leave to stand at room temperature for about 30 minutes.

Discard the bay leaf and brown the meat and garlic over moderate heat. Turn the beef to brown it evenly. Remove the garlic when it is brown, and reserve for later. Continue turning and browning the meat, covering it lightly in-between with paper to prevent splattering, until a meat thermometer registers 60 °C for medium-rare meat. It will take about 20–25 minutes, depending on the thickness of the cut.

Return the reserved garlic to the pot, cover the pot with a lid and remove the pot from the heat for 20 minutes. By this time you will have a small amount of the most delicious gravy in the pot. Carve the meat into thin slices and serve with the pan juices and roasted cloves of garlic.

This is delicious when served with polenta or baby potatoes and a green salad.

OVEN-SMOKED PEPPERED BEEF WITH BASIL SAUCE

SERVES 6

Smoking adds depth and flavour to food and this easy oven method gives excellent results. Most hardware stores and sports shops sell sawdust, and your hardware store should be able to cut the oak planks to size for you. The second plank is for turning.

FOR SMOKING
3 T (45 ml) oak sawdust
2 untreated oak planks, about 30 cm long and 18 cm wide
1 old cake tin

1 kg middle-cut beef fillet or rolled sirloin
3 T (45 ml) olive oil
2 T (30 ml) crushed black peppercorns
1 cup (250 ml) cream
3 T (45 ml) basil pesto
fresh basil for garnishing

Soak the wooden boards for at least an hour in water to which you have added lemon slices. Preheat the oven on conventional top and bottom heat (do not use the fan) to 250 °C.

Tie the meat with string to keep it neat, then brush it with olive oil and roll it in the crushed black peppercorns. Place it on one of the wet planks.

Place the cake tin with the sawdust in it on the shelf in the oven directly below the middle shelf. Wait about 5 minutes until the sawdust starts to smoke lightly. Place the meat, on the plank, on the middle shelf directly above the sawdust tray. Do not open the oven for 20 minutes.

Tumble-turn the meat onto the second wet plank and cook for 10 minutes or until the temperature registers medium-rare (60 °C) on a meat thermometer. Remove the meat from the oven, cover it lightly and leave it to rest on the plank for 10 minutes while you make the sauce.

Pour the cream into a saucepan. Cook over high heat until reduced. Add the basil pesto and taste for seasoning.

Slice the meat and serve hot with the sauce. Garnish with fresh basil if available. Alternatively, it is equally good served at room temperature. Reheat the sauce and serve the hot sauce with the meat.

DELICIOUS OXTAIL WITH TOMATO

SERVES 5–6

We have used beef shin with the oxtail to make the recipe more economical, but 2 oxtails could be used.

1 oxtail, excess fat removed
300–500 g beef shin
seasoned sea salt or garlic and herb seasoning
2 onions, chopped
2 carrots, chopped
4 cloves garlic, crushed
a handful of parsley
2 cups (500 ml) chicken or vegetable stock
1 packet (200 ml) sun-dried tomato Coat & Cook sauce
or 2 cups (500 ml) chopped fresh tomatoes
2–3 potatoes, peeled and diced

Season the meat with the salt or seasoning mix and combine it with the onions, carrots, garlic and parsley. In a heavybased, medium-sized saucepan heat the stock and tomato and add the meat and vegetables. Simmer very slowly for about 3 hours. Add the diced potato about 30 minutes before the end of the cooking time. To serve, sprinkle over some more chopped, fresh parsley and serve with rice and green vegetables, or a salad.

VARIATION
Use a whole brisket, beef topside or thick rib instead of oxtail.

MARINATED LEG OF WARTHOG

SERVES 8

This is a typically South African recipe, which one of our Burger readers was adamant we should include in this book! The leg has to be marinated overnight.

2½ t (12.5 ml) garlic and herb seasoning
1 t (5 ml) ground cloves
5 t (25 ml) vegetable stock powder
5 t (25 ml) seasoned sea salt
1 t (5 ml) ground ginger
black pepper
500 g rindless streaky bacon
1 leg of warthog
peel of 1 naartjie
½ cup (125 ml) apple juice
½ cup (125 ml) Coke
4 T (60 ml) marmalade

Mix together all the dry ingredients and roll the bacon rashers in the seasoning. Lard the warthog leg first with a piece of naartjie peel and then with the seasoned bacon rashers. Place the leg in the apple juice and marinate for 24 hours in the refrigerator.

When you are ready to cook the leg, preheat the oven to 160 °C. Place the leg with the apple juice in a heavybased saucepan and add the Coke. Cover with the lid and bake slowly for about 4 hours until tender and cooked (the time depends on the size of the leg). Baste from time to time with the gravy until the leg is nicely browned. Spread the marmalade over the leg and return it to the oven, without the lid. Increase the heat to 200 °C and roast for another 20–30 minutes to brown.

VARIATIONS
- Use an ordinary leg of pork and prepare in the same way.
- Use a springbok or blesbok leg instead of the warthog, and use lemon and herb basting sauce instead of the apple marinade.

glazed ham with roasted stuffed apples

GLAZED HAM
WITH ROASTED STUFFED APPLES

SERVES 6–8

A few year's ago we cooked about 5 hams, using different methods, and this one was the best. Prepare it in the evening and let it stand overnight, ready to glaze in the morning.

1.5 kg uncooked, boneless gammon
2 sticks celery
1 bay leaf
1 t (5 ml) black peppercorns
2 carrots, sliced
1 onion, cut into wedges
2 cups (500 ml) red wine or beer
½ cup (120 g) soft brown sugar
5 whole cloves
water to cover
extra whole cloves
4 T (60 ml) wholegrain mustard
½ cup (120 g) soft brown sugar

Place the meat in a heavybased pot with a snug-fitting lid, deep enough for the lid to close tightly. Add all the remaining ingredients, except for the mustard, the final ½ cup (125 ml) of sugar and the extra cloves. Cover and bring the gammon to a slow boil on top of the stove for 1 hour.

Remove the saucepan from the heat and wrap the saucepan first in a thick layer of newspaper and then in a thick blanket, duvet or sleeping bag. Set aside for 6 hours. (If you are using 3–5 kg ham, leave it for 10 hours, or 12 hours for a 7 kg ham.)

Preheat the oven to 200 °C. Remove the ham from the cooking liquid. Using a small, sharp knife, remove the skin, leaving the fat layer. Slice into the fat layer to form a diamond pattern and stud it with extra cloves. Spread the mustard over the ham and press brown sugar into the mustard. Bake until the sugar layer turns caramel brown.

Serve warm or at room temperature.

ROASTED STUFFED APPLES

6 smallish red apples (Starking, Top Red or Gala)
melted butter
250 g good quality pork sausages
2 slices crustless white bread
⅓ cup (80 ml) chicken stock
2 T (30 ml) chopped parsley
1 T (15 ml) chopped fresh thyme or 1 t (5 ml) dried thyme
12 pecan nuts, chopped

Preheat the oven to 200 °C. Slice the apples in half. Remove the pips and a small amount of flesh with a melon-baller, making small hollows. Brush the cut side of the apples with the melted butter. Slash the sausage casings and mix the meat with the bread, softened in the chicken stock. Add parsley and thyme.

Divide the stuffing between the apples, pushing it very firmly into the hollows, rounding it nicely over the tops. Sprinkle with nuts and place the apple halves on an oven tray. Bake for about 35 minutes. Serve garnished with a herb sprig.

SPRINGBOK POT ROAST WITH OLIVES

SERVES 8

The long, slow cooking method gives this dish the depth and richness one craves during the cold winter months.

1.5 kg springbok shoulder or leg
3 T (45 ml) red wine vinegar
2 t (10 ml) seasoned sea salt
2 T (30 ml) flour
3 T (45 ml) olive oil
3 sticks celery, diced
5 cloves garlic, sliced
2 T (30 ml) tomato pesto or tomato paste
1 x 400 g tin tomatoes
1 cup (250 ml) red wine
1 cup (250 ml) vegetable stock
1 cup (250 ml) green olives, stoned
½ cup (125 ml) raisins
2 T (30 ml) chopped fresh parsley

Rub the meat all over with the vinegar, cover and leave for a few hours at room temperature. Drain, pat dry with paper towel, season and dust with flour.

Heat the olive oil in a heavybased saucepan and brown the meat. Remove the meat and set aside. Add the celery, garlic, tomato pesto or paste, tomatoes and red wine. Boil fast without a lid until the wine has reduced by half. Add the vegetable stock and bring back to the boil. Add the browned meat. Bring to a simmer, cover with greaseproof paper and a lid and cook very gently for 2–2½ hours, until the meat is tender.

Add the olives, raisins and parsley and cook, uncovered, for a further 10 minutes before serving.

This is delicious served with wild rice and vegetables. I particularly love honeyed pumpkin (see page 89) with venison.

VENISON PIE

SERVES 10

This is one of my late mother, Nellie Jooste's, very best recipes. The venison needs to be marinated for 1 or 2 days beforehand, and if you are making your own pastry it is best made the night before.

1 x 1.5 kg venison shoulder or leg (in one piece)
1 cup (250 ml) buttermilk

2 lamb knuckles
1 T (15 ml) oil
garlic and herb seasoning
4 cups (1 litre) vegetable stock
1 onion, chopped
10 whole cloves, tied in a muslin bag
2 bay leaves
1 t (5 ml) ground coriander
1 T (15 ml) seasoned sea salt

SAUCE
2 onions, chopped
2 T (30 ml) oil
1 cup (250 ml) red wine (Pinotage)
½ cup (125 ml) wine vinegar
1 T (15 ml) Dijon mustard
2 T (30 ml) potato flour or cornflour

1 onion spiked with 4 whole cloves
½ egg, beaten

Remove the tough outer membrane from the meat. Coat the venison with buttermilk and marinate for 1–2 days in the fridge.

Dry the meat with paper towel and discard the buttermilk. Brown the lamb knuckles in oil in a large, heavybased saucepan. Remove with a slotted spoon, season with garlic and herb seasoning and set aside.

Brown the venison in the same pot, then remove and set aside. Season.

Pour off any excess oil. Add the rest of the ingredients to the saucepan and bring to the boil. Add the browned meat, cover with a tight-fitting lid and simmer gently until the meat is tender and begins to pull away from the bone (3–4 hours), or cover with foil or greaseproof paper and bake in a slow oven until done. Cool, remove bones, flake meat and reserve gravy.

To make the sauce, sauté the onions in fresh oil until golden. Add the wine and vinegar and boil rapidly over a very high heat until only about ½ cup (125 ml) of liquid remains. Add the reserved gravy and mustard. If there is less than 2 cups (500 ml) of sauce, add more water or stock. Thicken with potato flour, taste and adjust the seasoning. Add the flaked meat.

Preheat the oven to 200 °C.

Spoon the filling into a large pie dish. Place the onion spiked with 4 cloves in the middle of the meat to support the pastry. Cover with a layer of pastry, decorate with pastry strips and cut-outs. (It will freeze well up to this stage.) Brush the pastry with the beaten egg and bake at 200 °C for 45 minutes.

SOUR CREAM PASTRY
3 cups (360 g) bread flour
1 t (5 ml) salt
250 g unsalted butter
1 cup (250 ml) sour cream

Sift the flour and salt twice. Use a pastry blender and blend in the butter until it is the size of small peas. Add the sour cream and mix to a firm dough, using a small sharp knife. Knead a little. Roll and fold three times. Rest in the refrigerator overnight. Roll twice more and use.

STUFFED SWEET PEPPERS

SERVES 4

This is an absolutely delicious middle-of-the-week dish.

4 sweet peppers
5 T (75 ml) olive oil
3 whole cloves garlic
4 anchovy fillets
200 g minced beef or veal
salt and pepper
2 eggs, beaten
1 T (15 ml) capers
½ cup (125 ml) cubed mozzarella cheese
2 T (30 ml) grated pecorino cheese
1 t (5 ml) dried basil
½ t (2.5 ml) dried origanum
dried breadcrumbs

Preheat the oven to 180 °C. Halve the sweet peppers lengthways and remove the seeds. Heat the olive oil in a frying pan and sauté the garlic and anchovies. Remove the garlic as soon as it starts to brown and add the meat to the pan. Stir-fry and season with salt and pepper.

As soon as the meat is done and has absorbed all the flavourings, place it in a mixing bowl and allow it to cool slightly. Add the eggs, capers, mozzarella, pecorino and basil. Combine the ingredients and stuff the sweet peppers with the mixture.

Place the halved peppers on a greased baking sheet, sprinkle with origanum and breadcrumbs and bake for 30 minutes.

spaghetti with roasted cherry tomatoes

'When love and skill work together,

expect a masterpiece.'

John Ruskin

PASTA

SPAGHETTI WITH ROASTED CHERRY TOMATOES

SERVES 4

This is a superb recipe. January and February are the best months for tomatoes in South Africa.

750 g cherry tomatoes, halved
2 t (10 ml) seasoned sea salt
1 t (5 ml) sugar
1–2 red chillies, thinly sliced
4 cloves garlic, cut lengthways into strips
⅓ cup (80 ml) olive oil
8 sun-dried tomato quarters in vinaigrette
400 g spaghetti
salted boiling water
½ cup (125 ml) chopped fresh herbs (basil, marjoram, mint or parsley)
½ cup (125 ml) grated cheese (Parmesan, pecorino or mozzarella)

Preheat the oven to 220 °C. Season the halved tomatoes with seasoned sea salt and sugar and spread them out in a single layer on a baking sheet. Bake for 20–25 minutes. Toss with the chillies, garlic and olive oil. Make sure that all the delicious tomato juices are incorporated. Drain the sun-dried tomato quarters, halve them and add them to the roasted cherry tomatoes.

Boil the spaghetti in salted water according to the instructions on the packet, then drain. Toss the tomato mixture and fresh herbs lightly with the pasta and sprinkle liberally with cheese.

Serve with a green salad, fresh bread and a good red wine.

ITALIAN AUBERGINE ROLLS WITH PASTA

SERVES 6

This is a lovely recipe that I learned while doing a cooking course in the north of Italy. The rolls can be prepared a few hours in advance and baked just before serving.

2–3 medium to large aubergines
seasoned sea salt
olive oil
2 T (30 ml) tomato or basil pesto
basil leaves
250 g fresh egg tagliatelle
salted boiling water
4 T (60 ml) olive oil
1 t (5 ml) garlic and herb seasoning
½ cup (125 ml) grated Parmesan cheese

Preheat the oven to 180 °C. Slice the aubergines lengthways into slices 5 mm thick. Sprinkle with salt and leave to drain in a colander for 20 minutes. Pat dry and brush with olive oil. Bake for 30 minutes in a single layer on a baking sheet until brown on top. Spread the aubergine slices with tomato or basil pesto and top each slice with a fresh basil leaf.

Cook the pasta in boiling salted water until *al dente* (tender but still firm). Drain in a colander and toss with olive oil, seasoning and cheese.

Divide the pasta between the aubergine slices and roll them up. Place each aubergine 'parcel' join-side down on a greased baking sheet.

To serve, bake at 200 °C for 15 minutes to warm through.

Serve with a good green salad and Italian bread.

PASTA AND EGG BAKE

SERVES 4

*Use a little leftover pasta (any kind, with or without
a sauce) in this delectable dish.*

4 eggs
Parmesan or pecorino cheese, grated
salt and pepper
200 g cooked pasta
1 sprig parsley, chopped
olive oil

Beat the eggs in a mixing bowl. Sprinkle over the cheese, salt
and pepper and add the pasta (stir the pasta to loosen if the
strands stick together). Add the parsley and stir. Set aside to rest
for 10 minutes.

Heat the olive oil in a frying pan and spoon in the mixture.
Reduce the heat and leave until the eggs just set. Brown the top
under a heated grill. A delicious crust will form here and there on
the pasta.Cut into generous triangular pieces for serving.

TAGLIARINI
WITH GARLIC AND OLIVE OIL

SERVES 4

*Tagliatelli or spaghetti would be equally good in this easy,
delicious recipe.*

250 g tagliarini
salted boiling water
3 large cloves garlic, cut into strips
6 T (90 ml) olive oil
2 or 3 red chillies, cut into thin rings, seeds included
a handful of parsley, chopped

Boil the pasta in salted water until *al dente*. Drain, reserving
4 T (60 ml) water for later. Meanwhile, fry the garlic slowly in the
olive oil in a frying pan. Add the chillies and half of the parsley
as soon as the garlic starts to change colour. Increase the heat,
add the pasta and heat with the reserved water in which the
pasta was boiled.

Sprinkle the rest of the parsley over and serve immediately.

SPAGHETTI WITH BACON AND EGGS

SERVES 4

*This is always a hit, and one usually has most of the
ingredients available.*

350 g spaghetti
boiling salted water
6 rashers rindless bacon, diced
2 egg yolks
grated pecorino or ripe, sharp provolone cheese
freshly ground black pepper

Boil the spaghetti until *al dente*, according to the instructions on
the packet. Meanwhile, put a few drops of water in a frying pan
and fry the bacon. Beat the egg yolks with the grated cheese in
a large mixing bowl and grind the black pepper over. Drain the
spaghetti well, combine with the egg and cheese mixture in the
mixing bowl, add the bacon and stir it through. The heat of the
spaghetti will cook the eggs. When serving, sprinkle extra
cheese over, to taste.

MACARONI
WITH AUBERGINES AND RICOTTA

SERVES 4–6

This is the perfect dish for a Sunday evening.
Aubergines are reputed to be good for the heart, so consider
this dish a healthy option.

2 aubergines, sliced
6 T (90 ml) olive oil
1 clove garlic
6 ripe tomatoes or 1 x 410 g tin whole peeled tomatoes,
coarsely chopped
400 g macaroni
boiling salted water
salt and pepper
½ cup (125 ml) ricotta cheese
fresh basil, chopped

Salt the aubergine slices and leave to drain in a colander for 20 minutes. Rinse them, pat them dry and then cut them into cubes. Sauté them with the olive oil and garlic in a frying pan. Remove from the stove and spoon into a mixing bowl.

If you are using fresh tomatoes, skin them by soaking them first for a few minutes in boiling water to loosen the skins. Sauté the chopped tomato in the frying pan for 10 minutes, then combine them with the aubergines.

Boil the macaroni in salted water until *al dente*. Drain and lightly toss with the vegetables in the mixing bowl. Add the salt, pepper, cheese and basil. Stir through and serve hot.

BAKED PASTA
WITH CAULIFLOWER AND CHEESE

SERVES 4 AS A MAIN COURSE OR 6 AS A SIDE DISH

This family favourite is good served during the colder months
as a vegetarian main course or as a side dish to complement
grilled or roast poultry, or fish.

1 medium cauliflower, broken into florets
1½ cups (375 ml) screw pasta
boiling salted water
½ cup (125 ml) chopped onion
3 T (45 ml) butter
3 T (45 ml) flour
2 cups (500 ml) full cream milk
½ t (2.5 ml) salt
freshly ground black pepper
grated nutmeg
½ cup (125 ml) crumbled feta cheese
½ cup (125 ml) plain low fat cottage cheese
4 T (60 ml) grated Emmenthaler or good Gouda cheese
4 T (60 ml) fresh breadcrumbs

Preheat the oven to 190 °C. Steam the cauliflower until just soft. Bring a pot of salted water to the boil, add the pasta and cook it until *al dente*. Drain the pasta and toss it with the cauliflower. Sauté the onion slowly in the butter for a few minutes. Add the flour and cook for 1–2 minutes, stirring continuously. Slowly add the milk and keep stirring to make a white sauce. Season the sauce with salt, pepper and nutmeg. Add the feta and cottage cheese. Toss the pasta and cauliflower mixture with the sauce and dish into a lightly oiled casserole dish. Combine the grated Emmenthaler or Gouda cheese and the fresh breadcrumbs and sprinkle on top. Bake for 30 minutes.

VARIATION
Use 300–400 g sliced courgettes in place of the cauliflower.

italian aubergine rolls with pasta

capelli d'angelo with seafood

CAPELLI D'ANGELO (ANGELHAIR PASTA) WITH SEAFOOD

SERVES 6

*I'd place this recipe in the
'restaurant eating at home' category.*

RED WINE AND TOMATO SAUCE
6 T (60 ml) olive oil
1 celery bulb, sliced
4 T (60 ml) coarsely chopped parsley
½ cup (125 ml) chopped onion
3 cloves garlic, crushed
½ cup (125 ml) grated carrot
½ cup (125 ml) red wine
1½ t (7.5 ml) garlic and herb seasoning
½ t (2.5 ml) cayenne pepper or Tabasco sauce
sugar to taste
2 T (30 ml) tomato pesto
freshly ground black pepper
sugar to taste
5 ripe tomatoes, skinned and chopped
1 T (15 ml) vegetable stock powder
1 cup (250 ml) water
500 g firm fish (kingklip, red roman, kabeljou), skinned and
cut into cubes
300 g prawns
300 g calamari rings
300 g shelled mussels
500 g capelli d'angelo (angelhair pasta)
salted boiling water

GREMOLADA
½ cup (125 ml) chopped parsley
2 T (30 ml) grated lemon rind
6 cloves garlic, crushed

To make the red wine and tomato sauce, sauté all the vegetables except for the tomatoes in the olive oil until tender and full of flavour. Soak the tomatoes in boiling water for a few minutes to loosen the skins, then peel and chop. Add the tomatoes and the rest of the ingredients and simmer slowly for about 20–30 minutes, until thick. Remove from heat and taste for seasoning. Set aside.

In a large saucepan, dissolve the stock powder in the water. Add the fish and simmer for 5 minutes. Add the prawns, calamari and mussels and cook for a further 2 minutes. Remove the seafood with a slotted spoon and add it to the red wine and tomato sauce. Add some of the stock to the sauce until the consistency of the sauce resembles thin cream. Taste for seasoning.

Cook the pasta until *al dente* in boiling, salted water according to the instructions on the packet. Drain.

Make the gremolada by simply mixing together the parsley, lemon rind and garlic.

Toss the pasta lightly with a little olive oil. Place it in a large serving dish and spoon over the seafood sauce and top with gremolada. Serve with salad and bread.

BABY ONION AND FRESH PEA RISOTTO

SERVES 4

Serve either as a starter or as a side dish.
It is excellent with chicken or lamb.

225 g baby onions, unpeeled but topped and tailed
4 T (60 g) butter
2 T (30 ml) olive oil
4 cloves garlic, peeled and sliced lengthways into
fine slivers
2 T (30 ml) chopped fresh sage
2 t (10 ml) soft brown sugar
1 t (5 ml) salt
freshly ground black pepper
1¼ cups (225 g) risotto or arborio rice
½ cup (125 ml) red wine
4 T (60 ml) ruby port (optional)
4 cups (I litre) hot vegetable stock
1 cup (250 ml) shelled fresh peas or frozen petits pois
1–2 T (15–30 ml) sun-dried tomato pesto or tomato paste
4 T (60 ml) freshly grated Parmesan or pecorino cheese
sage sprigs to garnish

Put the onions in a saucepan with cold water. Bring to the boil and simmer for 30 seconds, then drain and refresh under cold water. Peel away the skins and halve the onions if they are a bit large. Melt half the butter with the oil in a heavybased saucepan. Add the onions and garlic and fry over a medium heat for 5 minutes until the onions are caramelised. Stir in the sage, sugar, salt and pepper and shake the pan until the onions are glossy and cooked through. Remove from the heat.

Put the stock in a small pot and bring it to a simmer. Meanwhile, melt the remaining butter in a heavybased, non-stick frying pan. Add the rice and stir-fry for 1–2 minutes until all the grains are glossy and well coated. Add the wine, and Port if using, and boil rapidly until the liquid has been almost totally absorbed. Gradually add the simmering stock to the rice, a ladleful at a time, stirring the rice constantly and making sure each addition is absorbed before adding the next. Continue for about 20 minutes, until most of the stock has been added and the rice is almost cooked. Add the onion mixture to the rice with the remaining stock and the peas and continue to cook, stirring, until the liquid is absorbed and the rice is cooked, but firm.

Remove the pan from the heat and stir in the sun-dried tomato pesto and two-thirds of the Parmesan. Season, and allow the risotto to stand for 5 minutes, covered. Serve topped with the remaining Parmesan and garnished with sage.

VARIATION
The sage can be replaced with two-thirds origanum
or basil, and one-third rosemary.

SOUTH AFRICAN BASIL PESTO

MAKES 2 CUPS (500 ML)

*South Africa is a big producer of macadamia nuts. I find
their meaty, dense texture an excellent substitute for pine nuts,
which are exorbitantly expensive. In fact, the macadamias are
better in my book. By wilting the basil leaves first in oil, one
locks in the flavour and preserves the colour. The pesto can be
kept refrigerated for 1–2 weeks or frozen for 6 months.*

½ cup (50 g) macadamia nuts
2 cups (500 ml) tightly packed basil leaves and soft,
tender stems
6–8 cloves garlic
1 cup (250 ml) olive oil
4 T (60 ml) freshly grated Parmesan cheese
4 T (60 ml) grated pecorino romano cheese
1 t (5 ml) salt
freshly ground black pepper to taste

Sauté the nuts in about ¼ cup (62.5 ml) of the oil. Remove the
pan from the heat. Add the basil and turn the leaves in the oil.
Don't cook them; they must just wilt a little. Place the nuts, wilted
basil and garlic into a processor and process until smooth.
Slowly add the olive oil. When all the oil has been added, blend
in the cheeses and seasoning. Taste and adjust the seasoning.

WHOLEWHEAT PASTA
WITH TOMATO AND ROCKET SALAD

SERVES 4–6

*Rocket is a very easy herb to grow.
Its peppery taste is almost addictive. Young spinach leaves
can be used instead of rocket.*

300 g wholewheat noodles
6 T (90 ml) olive oil
4 fresh, ripe tomatoes, diced
2 packets (about 60 g) rocket, washed and chopped
salt and pepper

Boil the noodles in salted water until *al dente*, then drain. Pour
the olive oil into a saucepan and stir-fry the tomato, rocket, salt
and pepper for 1 minute. Toss this sauce into the pasta and heat
it gently. Serve with Parmesan cheese.

PESTO ERICINESE

SERVES 4

*Pesto Ericinese is the Sicilians' version of the more famous
Genoese pesto, using almonds rather than pine nuts and
tomatoes. Toss it into piping hot pasta.*

1 cup (250 ml) fresh basil leaves
3 cloves garlic, roughly chopped
½ t (2.5 ml) salt
freshly ground black pepper
1 cup (100 g) blanched almonds
½ cup (125 ml) freshly grated pecorino or Parmesan cheese
3 large tomatoes
1 T (15 ml) tomato paste
1 t (5 ml) sugar
⅓ cup (80 ml) olive oil

Pour boiling water over the tomatoes to loosen the skins. Peel,
seed and roughly chop them. Place the basil leaves, garlic, salt,
pepper, almonds and cheese in the processor and process to a
rough paste. Add the tomatoes, tomato paste and sugar and
process again, gradually trickling in the olive oil. Taste and add
more salt and pepper if necessary. This pesto will keep for up to
a week in an airtight container in the fridge.

courgette carpaccio salad

'Don't trust your most valuable

possession, good health, to anybody

but Mother Nature.'

Unknown

SALADS

COURGETTE CARPACCIO SALAD

SERVES 4–6

This salad makes a stunning visual display,
either on a salad platter to serve with a main meal,
or on individual plates, served as a starter.

8 courgettes, washed, topped and tailed
3 T (45 ml) extra virgin olive oil
1 t (5 ml) Balsamic vinegar
salt
freshly ground black pepper
1 packet (about 30 g) rocket leaves, washed, dried and
roughly torn
125 g Parmesan cheese

Slice the courgettes into paper-thin slices with a mandolin slicer or a very sharp small knife. Arrange in overlapping concentric circles on a flat platter or individual plates.

Drizzle with olive oil and vinegar and season with salt and freshly ground black pepper. Cover with clingfilm pressed flat so that the courgettes remain fresh and leave to stand for 1 hour. Top with rocket leaves and shavings of parmesan (use a cheese slicer or potato peeler), just before serving.

AVOCADO AND KIWI FRUIT SAMBAL

SERVES 4

This easy sambal is delicious served with a braai or a curry.

2 ripe kiwi fruit, peeled and diced
4 spring onions, thinly sliced
2 ripe tomatoes, diced
1 chilli, thinly sliced, with seeds
2 T (30 ml) lemon juice
1 ripe avocado, peeled and diced
seasoned sea salt to taste

Mix all the ingredients together lightly and serve.

ORANGE AND AVOCADO SALAD WITH BACON

SERVES 6

8 rashers meaty back bacon
2 large oranges, peeled
1 butter lettuce
2 ripe avocados
4 T (60 ml) lite French dressing
parsley or mint, chopped

Cut the bacon into strips and grill until crispy. Remove the orange segments using a sharp knife. Slice the outer leaves of the lettuce into fine strips. Arrange the remaining leaves and the orange segments in a fan shape on individual salad plates. Peel the avocados, stone and dice. Toss with the dressing and sliced lettuce and add to the salad on each plate. Top each one with bacon. Sprinkle over a little parsley or mint if desired.

SWEET POTATO AND SNOEK SALAD

Sweet potatoes and snoek with a sweet mustard dressing is a combination made in heaven and quintessentially South African. You'll also like this time-saving, never-fail technique for cooking sweet potatoes. This is a filling salad suitable for a main course.

3 medium sweet potatoes
½ cup (125 ml) honey mustard dressing
seasoned sea salt to taste
1 butter lettuce
800 g smoked snoek, flaked and deboned
½ cup (125 ml) thinly sliced spring onions with green tops

Preheat the oven to 180 °C. Peel the sweet potatoes and cut into 1 cm cubes. Place in a large bowl and add just enough dressing to lightly coat the cubes. Season with seasoned salt and toss. Arrange the sweet potatoes in a single layer in a swiss roll pan. Bake for about 20 minutes until tender. Allow to cool.

Line individual serving plates with butter lettuce. Place a layer of flaked and deboned smoked snoek on top, then add the sweet potatoes and spring onions. Coat with extra dressing. Serve with country bread and fresh fruit.

VARIATION
Use 500 g shaved turkey or ham in place of snoek.

PEAR SALAD
WITH BLUE CHEESE CROUTONS

This makes a delicious starter.

4–6 slices wholewheat bread
olive oil or butter
50 g creamy blue cheese
2 T (30 ml) coarsely chopped pecan nuts
1 firm, ripe pear
4 T (60 ml) lemon juice
¼ crisp lettuce (butter or cos lettuce)
2 sticks celery, thinly sliced
1 x 50 g packet honey mustard salad dressing, or make your own salad dressing

Preheat the oven to 200 °C. Using a round biscuit cutter 5 cm in diameter, cut out rounds from the bread. Brush both sides lightly with olive oil or spread with butter and bake for 10 minutes until crisp. Allow to cool.

Mash the cheese, adding a little milk if it is very dry. Spread a thick layer of cheese over each crouton. Sprinkle with half the nuts. Cut the unpeeled pear lengthways into slices and discard the pips. Dip lightly in lemon juice diluted half-and-half with water. Arrange the lettuce leaves on individual plates and top with the pear slices. Place 1 or 2 cheese toasts on each plate and sprinkle with the sliced celery and remaining nuts. Pour salad dressing over and serve.

LENTIL SALAD WITH FETA

SERVES 6–8

*There is something so satisfying and health giving about a
lentil salad. This is one of my favourites.
It keeps well in the fridge.*

1 cup (250 ml) red lentils
2½ cups (625 ml) vegetable stock
3 cloves garlic, crushed
4 spring onions with green tops, finely sliced
1 small English cucumber, diced
200 g cherry tomatoes, halved
2 T (30 ml) chopped parsley
2 rounds feta cheese, diced
½ cup (125 ml) herb or garlic dressing

Boil the lentils in the stock for 12–17 minutes until done. Drain
and cool. Mix the garlic, spring onions, cucumber, tomatoes and
parsley. Cover and refrigerate until ready to serve.

To serve, combine the cooled lentils with the prepared salad
ingredients and diced feta. Toss with the dressing of your choice.

VARIATION
Cook the lentils with 1 t (5 ml) cumin. It imparts an
excellent flavour.

SALAD OF PATTY PANS AND TOMATO

SERVES 4

*This unusual salad has great colour contrast and is easy
to put together.*

300 g yellow or green patty pan squashes
2 T (30 ml) chopped fresh origanum or fresh
basil or parsley
4 T (60 ml) honey mustard dressing
200 g cherry tomatoes
grated rind of 1 lemon
seasoned sea salt
freshly ground black pepper
fresh herbs for garnishing (basil, origanum,
marjoram or parsley)

Cut the patty pans into eighths. Mix the herbs with the dressing.
Pour the dressing over the patty pans and allow to stand for
approximately 35 minutes.

Cut the tomatoes in half and arrange on 4 medium-sized
plates. Scatter the grated lemon rind over the tomatoes and
season with salt and freshly ground black pepper.

Spoon a pile of patty pan pieces in the centre of each plate of
tomatoes, garnish with fresh herbs, and serve.

salad of patty pans and tomato

ROASTED ONION SALAD WITH ANCHOVIES AND BLACK OLIVES

SERVES 8

This robust salad complements braaied fish, chicken or beef beautifully.

6 large onions, peeled and cut into 1 cm thick slices
½ cup (125 ml) garlic dressing
1 t (5 ml) seasoned sea salt
1 small tin rolled anchovy fillets (reserve oil)
1 cup (250 ml) Calamata olives, stoned
1 butter lettuce

Preheat the oven to 250 °C. Toss the onion slices with the dressing, salt and the reserved oil from the anchovies. Spread out in a single layer on a baking pan. Roast for 45 minutes until the onions are soft and brown. Toss the roasted onion with the anchovies and olives. Keep refrigerated until you are ready to serve. Spoon onto a bed of lettuce and serve.

MUSTARD ONION SALAD

SERVES 8–10

1 kg pickling onions, peeled
2 cups (500 ml) chicken or vegetable stock
1 cup (250 ml) red wine or brown malt vinegar
2 T (30 ml) cornflour or potato flour
4 T (60 ml) brown sugar
2 eggs
2 t (10 ml) mustard powder
1 t (5 ml) seasoned sea salt

Simmer the onions in the stock until tender. Remove with a slotted spoon and set aside in a serving dish while you make the sauce.

Add the wine or vinegar to the stock. Blend the cornflour with a little water and add. Beat the sugar, eggs, mustard powder and salt together. Add a little of the hot mixture to the egg mixture and then pour all the egg mixture into the saucepan. Stir continuously over a gentle heat, with a whisk, until the sauce thickens. Adjust the seasoning to taste. Pour over the onions and leave to cool.

BAKED BEETROOT SALAD WITH RAISINS AND CORIANDER

SERVES 4–5

This recipe was very enthusiastically received by my Burger *readers! Beetroot baked slowly in the oven has a much more intense flavour than boiled beetroot. This salad is excellent with chicken or pork, or roast leg of lamb.*

6 medium beetroot, washed
½ cup (85 g) seedless raisins, rinsed with boiling water
1 medium onion, finely chopped
2 cloves garlic, bruised
4 T (60 ml) finely chopped parsley
4 T (60 ml) coriander leaves
4 T (60 ml) low-oil French salad dressing

Preheat the oven to 180 °C. Place the whole, unpeeled beetroot in a single layer in a baking dish and bake, uncovered, for an hour. Allow to cool, then peel and dice into fairly small pieces. Combine with the raisins, onion, garlic, parsley, coriander and salad dressing, and serve.

CREAMY BEETROOT RING

SERVES 6–8

*Beetroot has great depth of flavour and a marvellous colour;
dressed up, it can make a real statement.
This is excellent for a fish buffet.*

4 fairly large beetroot
2 t (10 ml) vegetable or chicken stock
4 t (20 ml) gelatine
½ cup (125 ml) boiling water
1 cup (250 ml) mayonnaise
1 small onion, chopped
1 t (5 ml) seasoned sea salt
2 t (10 ml) sugar
2 T (30 ml) lemon juice
1 cup (250 ml) whipped cream

GARNISH
lettuce leaves
avocado
fresh herbs

Boil the beetroot until tender, then peel and dice. Place in a food processor. Sprinkle the gelatine powder over 4 T (60 ml) cold water and set aside for a few minutes until spongy. Dissolve the stock powder and gelatine in the boiling water. Add to the beetroot and process until smooth. Add the mayonnaise, onion, salt, sugar and lemon juice. Allow to cool in the refrigerator until it just begins to set. Fold in the whipped cream and pour into a ring mould dipped first in water to dampen.

Refrigerate overnight to set. Turn out and decorate with lettuce leaves, avocado slices and fresh herbs.

COOK'S TIPS
The best way to cook beetroot is to bake it in the oven until it is soft, rather than the more conventional method of boiling.
Leave about 5 cm of the stems intact to lessen the colour loss.

TOASTED TUSCAN BREAD SALAD WITH TOMATOES AND BASIL

SERVES 4

*This is an ideal main course salad to enjoy alfresco on a
summer's evening with a crisp, cold white wine.*

½ ciabatta (Italian bread)
500 g ripe fresh plum or cherry tomatoes
2 T (30 ml) good quality red wine vinegar
2 cloves garlic, crushed
½ cup (125 ml) extra virgin olive oil
seasoned sea salt
freshly ground black pepper
a handful fresh basil leaves
juice of half a lemon

Preheat the oven to 240 °C. Roughly tear the loaf into eighths and place on a baking tray. Bake in the oven for about 5–10 minutes until dry and toasted on the outside, but soft in the centre. Place in a bowl.

Cut 4 of the tomatoes in half through the middle and, using your hands, squeeze them over the toasted bread. Mix together a dressing using the vinegar, garlic and half the olive oil, and season with salt and pepper. Pour the dressing over the toasted bread and tomato and toss. Skin and seed the remaining tomatoes (see Cook's tip), slice lengthways into eighths and add, with the basil, to the bread mixture. Finally, add the lemon juice to bring out the flavour of the tomatoes, and pour over the remaining olive oil.

COOK'S TIP
The retained tomato juices and seeds are delicious tossed with *al dente* pasta together with 1 T (15 ml) tomato pesto and chopped fresh origanum or basil.

pita bread salad with blue cheese dressing

PITA BREAD SALAD
WITH BLUE CHEESE DRESSING

SERVES 6

3 pita breads (saucer size)
olive oil
garlic and herb seasoning
200 g cherry tomatoes, halved
½ cup (125 ml) chopped parsley
½ cup (125 ml) chopped fresh mint
1 bunch spring onions with green tops, finely sliced,
1 English cucumber, diced
1 green pepper, finely diced
1 butter lettuce, washed and crisped
½ cup (125 ml) blue cheese dressing
1 small onion, cut into rings

Preheat the oven to 200 °C. Split the pita breads in half to expose the soft insides. Brush the soft sides with olive oil and sprinkle lightly with seasoning. Arrange on a baking sheet, oiled sides up. Bake for 20 minutes until toasted a golden brown. Remove from the oven and leave to cool a little. Break into bite-size pieces. (Keep these in an airtight container if you are going to serve the salad later and are preparing in advance.)

Toss the tomatoes, parsley, mint, spring onions, cucumber and green pepper together. (Keep these covered in the fridge until serving time if done in advance.)

To serve, line individual salad plates with torn lettuce leaves. Carefully toss the bread with the prepared vegetables and dressing and divide the mixture between the plates. Top with onion rings and serve.

PINEAPPLE AND PICCALILLI
LONG LIFE SALAD

This quick and easy salad goes well with grilled chicken or pork. It keeps for up to week in an airtight container in the fridge.

1 x 400 g tin pineapple pieces
1 x 390 g jar piccalilli
4 T (60 ml) good quality mayonnaise
4 spring onions, finely sliced

Drain the juice off the pineapple pieces and reserve a little. Mix all the ingredients together and add a little of the pineapple syrup if it is too dry.

MARINATED MUSHROOM SALAD

SERVES 4

This country-style salad keeps in the refrigerator for up to a week and is a wonderful standby for braaied meat or with fish.

½ red pepper, diced small
½ yellow pepper, diced small
4 T (60 ml) olive oil
4 T (60 ml) water
4 T (60 ml) lemon juice or apple cider vinegar
1 bay leaf
4 cloves garlic, cut lengthways into thin strips
1 medium chilli, thinly sliced
2 t (10 ml) garlic and herb flavouring
250 g button mushrooms, wiped clean and halved
200 g oyster mushrooms, cut into thin strips

Boil everything together for 30 seconds.

NUTTY PASTA AND MUSHROOM SALAD WITH FETA AND YOGHURT DRESSING

SERVES 6

½ cup (50 g) whole pecan nuts
2 T (30 ml) Canola or olive oil
seasoned sea salt
1 cup (250 ml) raw farfalle or elbow macaroni
boiling salted water
1 cup (250 ml) blue cheese dressing
½ cup (125 ml) yoghurt
1 round crumbled feta cheese
250 g button mushrooms, sliced
salad leaves

Stir-fry the nuts in the Canola or olive oil until crisp and golden. Remove with a slotted spoon and drain on kitchen paper. Season and chop roughly.

Boil the pasta in the salted water until *al dente*. Drain and toss while still warm with the dressing, yoghurt, cheese and mushrooms. Leave until cool.

To serve, dish the pasta onto a bed of lettuce and top with the crispy salted nuts. Serve either on a large platter or on individual salad plates.

CHICKEN NOODLE SALAD

We are all looking for the ultimate chicken salad with noodles. Here it is, delicious, quite economical and lovely to look at.

SERVES 6–8

1 cup (250 ml) chicken stock
1 T (15 ml) tarragon or basil
2 t (10 ml) medium-strength curry powder
6–8 chicken breasts
garlic and herb seasoning
5 sticks celery, very finely sliced diagonally
1 bunch spring onion, very finely sliced diagonally
2 red-skinned apples, cored and thinly sliced
2½ cups (625 ml) cooked screw noodles
1 cup (250 ml) honey mustard dressing
salad greens
1 cup (250 ml) roughly chopped pecan nuts, toasted

Bring the chicken stock , tarragon and curry to the boil. Season chicken with garlic and herb seasoning, add the chicken breasts to the stock and turn the heat low. Cover and cook for 5–6 minutes only. Remove the pan from the stove and leave the chicken in the liquid to cool to room temperature.

Toss the celery with the spring onions and apples. Slice the chicken across the grain into 5 mm thick slices. Return it to the stock to soak up moisture for 5 minutes. Drain and toss the chicken and noodles in honey mustard dressing. Fold in celery, apples and spring onions. Place salad greens around edge of plate and pile chicken in the middle. Sprinkle over nuts. Serve with fresh home-made bread and butter, and one of the Cape's excellent Late Harvest Cape Wines, well chilled.

chicken noodle salad

mushrooms with man appeal and perfect chips

'*Charm:* The ability to make someone

think both of you are wonderful.'

Ambrose Bierce

VEGETABLES

MUSHROOMS WITH MAN APPEAL

SERVES 6

*The robust, meaty flavours and nutty crunch of this dish
will appeal even to men, who would normally not enjoy
a vegetarian main course.*

12 large black mushrooms
4 T (60 ml) olive oil
garlic and herb seasoning
4 T (60 ml) Parmesan or pecorino cheese, finely grated
⅓ cup (80 ml) drained sun-dried tomato quarters,
roughly chopped
½ cup (125 ml) soft fresh breadcrumbs
½ cup (50 g) cashew or macadamia nuts,
roughly chopped

Preheat the oven to 220 °C. Wipe the mushrooms clean with
damp kitchen paper. Cut the stems level with the mushrooms,
finely chop the stem pieces and reserve them for the topping.
Brush a large oven pan with some of the olive oil and arrange
the mushrooms, gills up, in the pan. Season the mushrooms and
top with the cheese. Mix the remaining olive oil with the chopped
mushroom stems, drained sun-dried tomatoes, breadcrumbs
and chopped cashew nuts. Toss to blend. Divide the mixture
between the mushroom caps. Bake for 20 minutes. Garnish with
fresh herbs and serve.

COOK'S TIP
Once the mushrooms have been seasoned they will start
drawing water, so this recipe can be prepared up to just before
baking stage only up to 2 hours in advance.

PERFECT CHIPS

SERVES 4

*To make chips that are crisp outside and soft inside, fry them
twice. The first time, they are just cooked; the second time they
turn pale golden brown and crisp. The quality of chips
depends on the freshness of the oil. Do not use oil more than
three times and never overheat it. Red-skinned potatoes are
perfectly suited for chips.*

6 large floury potatoes, preferably with
yellowish flesh, peeled
Canola oil
salt

Cut the potatoes into chips. Rinse them in cold water and pat
them dry with a clean drying cloth. Place enough oil in a deep
fryer to cover the chips and heat to about 180 °C (moderate
heat). Place the chips in a frying basket, lower it into the oil and
fry the chips until they are soft but not yet browned. Lift the chips
out of the oil and set them aside. Just before serving, place the
chips in the pan again and fry quickly until golden brown. Drain
well, sprinkle with salt and serve immediately.

VARIATION
For a special occasion, try frying the chips in olive oil.

BAKED BUTTERNUT CASSEROLE
WITH FETA CHEESE

SERVES 4

This is an excellent vegetarian dish.

1 medium butternut squash, peeled and diced
seasoned sea salt
2 T (30 ml) butter
½ cup (125 ml) cubed feta cheese
4 spring onions with green tops, thinly sliced
3 eggs, beaten
1 cup (250 ml) buttermilk, cream or sour cream

Preheat the oven to 180 °C. Steam the butternut until just tender. Season and add the butter. Mix with the feta cheese and spring onions.

Spoon the mixture into a medium-sized baking dish. Beat the eggs with the buttermilk, cream or sour cream and pour over the vegetables. Bake for 35–40 minutes, until nicely browned and puffed up. Serve with a tomato and onion salad and a crisp green salad.

VARIATION
Potatoes can be used instead of butternut.

COOK'S TIP
The easiest way to peel a butternut squash is with a potato peeler. Choose a butternut with a thick neck and a small base, as it will have more flesh.

IRISH MASHED POTATO
WITH CABBAGE

SERVES 6

Comfort food at its best. My husband is of Irish extract and this is one of his favourites.

5 large or 6 medium potatoes
4 T (60 ml) cream
4 T (60 ml) milk
2 T (30 ml) butter
white pepper and seasoned sea salt to taste
1 medium-sized green cabbage or 2 baby cabbages, finely shredded
1 T (15 ml) butter
1 bunch spring onions with green tops, finely sliced
2 T (30 ml) chopped parsley
seasoned sea salt to taste

Boil or steam the potatoes in their jackets until soft. Peel off the skins and put the potatoes through a potato ricer or mash them until smooth. Warm the cream, milk and butter together and beat into the potato. Season to taste with salt and pepper.

Steam the cabbage until soft but still bright green. Remove from the heat and add the butter, sliced spring onions, parsley and seasoning. Fold the cabbage into the potato and serve with any grilled or roast meat.

SWEET POTATO SWIRLS
WITH HONEY AND ORANGE

SERVES 8

*This delicious recipe has many advantages. It can be prepared
in advance – even the day before, it is neat and easy to dish
up, but best of all it brings all those wonderful old-fashioned
flavours of honey, butter, cinnamon and citrus back
to the modern dinner table.*

**4 medium-sized sweet potatoes, scrubbed, peeled
and sliced
4 T (60 ml) honey
2 T (30 ml) butter
4 T (60 ml) fresh orange juice
1 T (15 ml) fresh lemon juice
1 t (5 ml) grated orange rind
1 t (5 ml) seasoned sea salt
2 t (10 ml) custard powder, mixed with a little
of the orange juice
2 T (30 ml) orange liqueur (optional)
½ t (2.5 ml) ground cinnamon
1 egg, beaten
½ cup (125 ml) soft white breadcrumbs
2 small oranges, sliced 2 mm thick for presentation
pecan nut halves
small lemon leaves**

Steam the sweet potatoes until they are soft, then put them
through a potato ricer or mash them until smooth.

Warm the honey in a small saucepan or in the microwave.
Add the butter, orange juice (reserve a little for mixing with the
custard powder) and lemon juice, orange rind and seasoned
salt. Mix the custard powder with a little of the juice and thicken
the sauce with this.

Add the liqueur if desired, cinnamon, mashed sweet potato
and egg. Mix until blended. Add the breadcrumbs a spoonful at
a time until the mixture is thick enough to hold its shape when

piped. The amount of breadcrumbs will depend on the moisture
content of the individual sweet potatoes and the size of the egg.
Taste for seasoning.

Pipe a swirl of sweet potato on each orange slice and top with
a pecan nut. Arrange on a buttered baking sheet and keep
refrigerated until cooking time.

Preheat the oven to 220 °C and bake for 10–15 minutes until
just beginning to brown. Garnish with small lemon leaves.

Serve hot with roast lamb, chicken or venison pie. Steamed
green beans or wilted baby spinach would be a good choice for
a second vegetable.

COOK'S TIP
If you don't have custard powder you could use
cornflour to thicken the sauce.

MANGETOUT AND BABY PEAS

SERVES 6

*This deliciously sweet, fresh green dish is a particular
favourite with my family.*

**200 g mangetout or sugar snap peas, cut
into julienne strips
2 t (10 ml) olive oil
2 cups (500 ml) frozen petits pois
garlic and herb seasoning**

Toss the mangetout with the oil and steam or micro-steam for
5 minutes. Add the frozen baby peas or petits pois and steam for
a further 3 minutes. Season and serve.

VARIATION
Add chopped fresh mint.

sweet potato swirls with honey and orange

BRAISED CAULIFLOWER
WITH INDIAN SPICES

SERVES 4

A tasty vegetarian main course, also excellent as part
of a curry buffet.

1½ T (22.5 ml) Canola or sunflower oil
1 medium cauliflower, cut into florets
½ medium onion, thinly sliced
1 t (5 ml) ground cumin
1 t (5 ml) ground coriander
1 t (5 ml) ground turmeric
¼ t (1 ml) dried chilli
1 T (15 ml) fresh lemon juice
4 T (60 ml) Bulgarian yoghurt
4 T (60 ml) water
4 T (60 ml) fresh coriander leaves
½ cup (125 ml) frozen peas
garlic and herb flavouring to taste

Heat a large frying pan over moderate heat for about 3–4 minutes until very hot. Add the oil and tilt the pan so that the oil covers the base evenly. Sauté the cauliflower for 2–3 minutes until the florets just start to soften. Stir constantly. Add the onion and sauté for a further 4 minutes or so, until the cauliflower browns and the onions have softened.

Stir in the cumin, coriander, turmeric and chilli and sauté until the spices are toasted. Reduce the heat and add the lemon juice, yoghurt and water. Cover and simmer for 4 minutes to allow the flavours to blend. Add the coriander leaves and peas and stir lightly. Cover and simmer for about 2 minutes, until the cauliflower has softened completely but is still firm. Season. Serve with grilled fish or roast chicken or, for a vegetarian main course, with rice.

ROASTED ONION FLOWERS

SERVES 6–8

The flower shapes of these baked onions make
a lovely presentation.

16–20 small pickling onions, peeled
2 T (30 ml) sugar
1 cup (250 ml) chicken stock
2 T (30 ml) melted butter
chopped parsley

Preheat the oven to 200 °C. Cut the onions into chrysanthemum shapes by slicing into eighths down from the tops, but not right through, then opening them up to form petals. Place them snugly into a smallish ovenproof dish so that they support each other. Mix together the sugar, stock and melted butter and pour this over the onions. Cover the dish with wet greaseproof paper. Roast for 45 minutes. Sprinkle with chopped parsley and serve.

WATERBLOMMETJIES WITH HAZELNUTS

SERVES 6

A South African dish with a touch of class.

300 g fresh waterblommetjies
1 T (15 ml) olive oil
4 T (60 ml) chopped parsley
2 t (10 ml) grated lemon rind
½–1 t (2.5-5 ml) seasoned salt
½ cup (50 g) hazelnuts

Soak the waterblommetjies in salted water for 20–30 minutes. Drain. Break the waterblommetjies into smaller pieces. Toss with the olive oil. Steam or micro-steam until tender. Toss with the parsley, lemon rind and salt. They may be prepared in advance to this stage.

When ready to serve, reheat the waterblommetjies in the microwave. Toast the hazelnuts in a non-stick frying pan and chop them coarsely. Sprinkle on top of the waterblommetjies and serve.

MICROWAVE MEALIE MOULD

SERVES 4

This is an excellent recipe; one of those that really works well in the microwave.

4 mealies, cut off the cob
1 T (15 ml) butter
½ cup (125 ml) milk
seasoned sea salt
3 eggs, beaten
½ cup (125 ml) grated Cheddar cheese
½ cup (125 ml) soft white breadcrumbs
pinch of nutmeg
2 T (30 ml) chopped parsley or chives

Place the mealie kernels in a microwave dish with the butter and milk. Cover the dish. Microwave for 8 minutes on high (100 per cent). Spoon the mixture into a food processor and mix until smooth. Add the salt, eggs, cheese, breadcrumbs and nutmeg and mix well. Grease a microwave dish with butter.

Sprinkle parsley over the base. Place the dish in the refrigerator for a few minutes to allow the parsley to set. Spoon in the mealie mixture and smooth the top. Place on a rack in the microwave and microwave on medium (60 per cent power) for 12–15 minutes, depending on the depth of the dish. Turn out. Serve with braised tomatoes and onions seasoned with a pinch of chilli, as a vegetarian main course.

QUICK AND EASY POTATO PANCAKES

SERVES 4

We have these pancakes for breakfast every Sunday morning – but they are also delicious on special occasions with smoked salmon.

1 smallish onion, peeled
3 medium potatoes, peeled
1 egg
2 T (30 ml) flour
2 t (10 ml) garlic and herb seasoning
4–6 T (60–90 ml) oil

Chop the onion finely and place in a medium-size mixing bowl. Grate the potatoes on the coarse side of the grater and add to the onion. Add the egg and mix through. Add the flour and seasoning and mix until well blended.

Heat the oil in a large heavybased frying pan. Fry spoonfuls of the mixture in the hot oil, turning only once the one side is well browned. Cook the other side until done. Drain on kitchen paper towel. Keep the first batch in the oven at 180 °C while cooking the rest of the pancakes.

honeyed pumpkin

AUBERGINE ROLLS

SERVES 6

This dish with its robust Italian flavours is excellent as a vegetarian main course. Strict vegetarians can omit the anchovies and add another tablespoon of capers.

3 large aubergines
garlic dressing or olive oil
3 T (45 ml) olive oil
1 medium onion, finely chopped
3–4 ripe tomatoes, skinned and chopped
2 T (30 ml) sun-dried tomato pesto or tomato paste
3–4 cloves garlic, crushed
1 t (5 ml) dried basil
1 x 50 g tin anchovy fillets with the oil, chopped
1 T (15 ml) capers
½ cup (125 ml) grated mozzarella cheese
½ cup (125 ml) soft fresh breadcrumbs
4 T (60 ml) grated Parmesan or pecorino
fresh herbs, lightly chopped

Preheat the oven to 220 °C. Slice off the stem end of the aubergine and then slice lengthways into very thin slices (a bread or vegetable slicer works best). Brush the slices with garlic dressing or olive oil on both sides, lay them on a baking sheet and bake for 15 minutes until they have softened.

Place the olive oil and onion in a heavy pan, cover it with greaseproof paper well pressed down, as well as a lid. Sauté the onions very slowly over low to medium heat for 15 minutes. While you are doing this, skin the tomatoes by soaking them for a few minutes in boiling water to loosen the skins. Peel and chop, and add them with the tomato pesto to the sautéed onions. Cover and simmer for another 10 minutes until thick and pulpy. Taste and season. Remove the tomato mixture from the heat and add the garlic, basil, anchovy, capers and mozzarella cheese. Add the breadcrumbs.

Divide this mixture evenly between the roasted aubergine slices and roll them up like swiss rolls. Place the rolls with the joins facing down in an oiled ovenproof serving dish. Sprinkle grated Parmesan over the top. Bake, just before serving, for 20 minutes. Sprinkle with lightly chopped fresh herbs and serve immediately.

HONEYED PUMPKIN

SERVES 6–8

Forget about dieting for today – start the battle again tomorrow!

½ cup (125 ml) honey
6 T (90 ml) butter
stick of cinnamon
1 T (15 ml) lemon juice
1 kg flat white pumpkin, sliced and seeded (not peeled)
salt to taste

Boil the honey, butter, cinnamon stick and lemon juice in a shallow pan to form a thick syrup. Place the sliced pumpkin in the sauce. Cover with a lid and simmer slowly for 15 minutes. Turn the slices and simmer for another 15 minutes. Remove the lid. If a brown toffee syrup has not yet formed, leave it to cook for a few more minutes. Remove the cinnamon stick and serve hot, with every last drop of sauce from the pan.

BAKED PEPPERS
WITH TOMATOES AND OLIVES

SERVES 5–6

A good dish to serve either as a vegetarian main course,
or a vegetable side dish. I often serve it as a starter with
bruschetta or crostini before a light main course.

2 medium aubergines
1 t (5 ml) seasoned sea salt
3 red peppers, seeded and cut into eighths
3 yellow peppers, seeded and cut into eighths
1 x Marinate-in-a-Bag, Italian tomato flavour or sun-dried
tomato Coat & Cook sauce
2 T (30 ml) fresh basil or origanum, chopped
freshly ground black pepper
5 cloves garlic, cut into slivers lengthways
4 T (60 ml) olive oil
½ cup (125 ml) black Calamata olives, stoned
chopped parsley, for garnish
½ cup (125 ml) grated Parmesan cheese

Slice the aubergines into 1 cm thick rounds, and then into
fingers. Sprinkle them with salt and allow to stand for 30 minutes
in a colander to drain the juices. Rinse briefly.

Place the aubergines and peppers in the marinade, massage
gently and allow to marinate at room temperature for
30 minutes. Shake the vegetables and marinade out of the bag
into a medium-sized ovenproof dish.

Preheat the oven to 200 °C. Sprinkle over the basil or
origanum, freshly ground black pepper, garlic and olive oil. Don't
be concerned if the vegetables look too dry, for as the dish
bakes it draws its own juices from the peppers. Finally, sprinkle
over the olives and cover the dish with damp greaseproof or
brown paper – do not use foil. Bake for 50–60 minutes. Garnish
with parsley.

If you are serving it as a main dish, serve it hot and pass the
grated Parmesan around at the table.

SWEET-AND-SOUR PEARL ONIONS

SERVES 4–6

These sweet-and-sour baby onions are usually part
of an Italian antipasto selection. They are excellent with
braaied or cold meat and delicious with ham or mortadella.
Once cooked, they will keep, covered, in the
refrigerator for 3 or 4 days.

750 g pearl (baby) onions
boiling water
2 T (30 ml) olive oil
2 T (30 ml) tomato pesto or tomato paste
2 T (30 ml) sugar
3 T (45 ml) Balsamic vinegar
1 bay leaf
2 sprigs fresh thyme
salt and pepper
2 T (30 ml) chopped fresh parsley

To skin the onions, first top and tail them, then cover them with
boiling water. Leave for 1–2 minutes, then drain, rinse under
cold water and slip off the skins.

Warm the oil in a wide frying pan and add the onions. Shake
the pan to roll them and brown them, then add all the remaining
ingredients except for the parsley. Pour in enough water to cover
the onions. Bring to the boil, reduce the heat and cover. Simmer
gently for 40–45 minutes, shaking the pan occasionally, until the
onions are tender and bathed in a naturally thickened sweet-
and-sour sauce. Serve cold, sprinkled with parsley.

sweet-and-sour pearl onions

butterflied fish with red marinade

'There is a certain barbaric splendour

about a good barbecue which rises

above any other form of cooking.'

Savitri Bhatia, Shahi Turke, 1975

ALFRESCO

BUTTERFLIED FISH
WITH RED MARINADE

SERVES 6

This is one of my husband's favourite recipes. The marinade is robust in flavour and gives a good colour to the fish. It is best marinated well in advance on the day of cooking.

1 whole fish, about 1–2 kg (angelfish,
kabeljou or Cape salmon)
seasoned sea salt
freshly ground black pepper

RED MARINADE
seasoned sea salt
1½ t (7.5 ml) cayenne pepper
1 T (15 ml) paprika
1½ t (7.5 ml) freshly ground black pepper
1 chilli, finely sliced, with seeds
6 cloves garlic, crushed
½ cup (125 ml) sunflower or Canola oil

Mix all the ingredients for the red marinade to form an oily paste, preferably well in advance, to let the flavours develop. Butterfly the fish and remove the spine. Leave the skin on and, if you are using a large braai, leave the head and tail on. Slash the skin in a diamond pattern to prevent it from curling during cooking.

Season the fish and leave it in the fridge to firm. Just before cooking, stir the marinade to blend the oil with the other ingredients, and using a pastry brush, baste both sides of the fish with a generous amount of marinade. Clamp the fish in a braai grid and cook on the skin side first for about 7–10 minutes, until nicely browned. Then turn and cook on the fleshy side for 7–10 minutes, until cooked through. Test with a fork in the thickest part: the flesh should be white and just beginning to flake. One turn of the grid is quite enough. Serve with olive bread and salad.

FESTIVE FISH BRAAI

SERVES 6–8

Celebrate the holidays out of doors with a delectable fish braai.

1.3–1.6 kg fresh geelbek, yellowtail or steenbras
3–4 crayfish tails
12 large shrimps
seasoned sea salt

LEMON AND GARLIC MARINADE
½ cup (125 ml) olive oil
4 T (60 ml) lemon juice
2 t (10 ml) sugar
1 t (5 ml) salt
freshly ground black pepper
4 cloves garlic, crushed

Bone the fish and cut it into portions, leaving the skin on. Season thoroughly. Halve the crayfish tails and shrimps (from the head) lengthways. Remove the alimentary canals from both and rinse thoroughly. Season with seasoned sea salt. Place the fish and shellfish in a glass or porcelain dish.

Mix all the marinade ingredients together well and pour it over the fish and shellfish. Refrigerate until ready to use.

When you are ready to braai, remove the fish and shellfish from the marinade and thread the shrimps onto two thin kebab skewers to make them easier to turn. Place the fish and crayfish on the braai, and cook first on the flesh side and then on the skin side (or shell side) until just cooked. Add the shrimps only when you turn the fish over (turn it only once). Baste the fish and shellfish constantly with the marinade until they are cooked (the flesh of the fish should be white and just beginning to flake).

Serve with a green salad, potato salad and garlic bread.

PAELLA POTJIE

SERVES 8–10

Save this special recipe for when you have time to enjoy the
preparation and step-by-step cooking it involves.
It is well worth the effort.

meat tenderiser
350–500 g calamari rings
6–8 chicken drumsticks
4 T (60 ml) Canola oil
2 t (10 ml) garlic and herb seasoning
3 red peppers, sliced into quarters and seeded
1¼ cups (310 ml) raw long-grain rice
12 fat cloves garlic, slivered
½ cup (125 ml) dry white wine
2 cups (500 ml) chicken stock
1 x 410 g tin tomatoes, chopped
1 red chilli, sliced, with seeds
240 g sun-dried tomato quarters, drained of vinaigrette
1 cup (250 ml) black olives, stoned
½ cup (125 ml) olive oil
200–250 g headless prawns
750 g firm white fish (kingklip,
Cape salmon or yellowtail)
flour
250 g smoked mussels
extra olive oil

GREMOLADA TOPPING
4 T (60 ml) chopped fresh basil or origanum
1 T (15 ml) grated lemon rind
4–5 cloves garlic, crushed

Sprinkle the calamari with meat tenderiser and leave to stand for 20 minutes while you prepare the paella.

In a flat-bottomed, heavy cast-iron pot sauté the drumsticks in the oil until they are nicely browned. Turn the heat right down, cover the chicken with greaseproof paper well pushed down, and put the lid on. Sauté very slowly for 20–25 minutes. Remove the chicken with a slotted spoon and set aside. Season with the garlic and herb seasoning.

Turn the heat up and stir-fry the red peppers until soft. Remove and set aside. Stir-fry the rice in the same pot until glossy and golden. Add the garlic and stir through. Add the wine, stock, chopped tomatoes, sliced chilli, sun-dried tomatoes, olives and cooked drumsticks. Turn the heat right down to low, cover with greaseproof paper and cook for 20 minutes with the lid on. In the meantime, prepare the fish and seafood.

Rinse the calamari. Cut the fish into cubes and season. Heat a little of the olive oil in a large frying pan and stir-fry the prawn tails until just pink, then set aside. Add a little more oil to the pan and stir-fry the calamari. Set aside with the prawns. Dust the seasoned fish with a little flour, and add enough olive oil to the pan to stir-fry the fish. Don't overcook the fish; it should still be slightly underdone.

Arrange the prepared fish, seafood, smoked mussels and red peppers in a pretty pattern over the rice mixture in the pot. Season to taste. Cover with the lid and warm through for 5 minutes.

Prepare the gremolada topping by mixing together the chopped herbs, lemon rind and garlic. Drizzle a generous amount (½ cup (125 ml)) of olive oil over the paella and sprinkle over the gremolada topping. Serve with bread and a salad.

GRILLED NEW POTATOES
WITH ROSEMARY

SERVES 6

Skewered with a sprig of fragrant rosemary, then grilled, these
new potato sosaties are not only tasty, but look good and are
easy to handle. Serve them with grilled lamb or chicken, or
offer them as an appetiser with garlic mayonnaise.

1 kg new potatoes, well scrubbed
1 T (15 ml) seasoned sea salt
½ cup (125 ml) garlic dressing
2 T (30 ml) chopped fresh rosemary leaves
sprigs of rosemary
freshly ground black pepper to taste
6 or 12 kebab skewers

In a medium saucepan, cover the potatoes with cold water. Set
over high heat, add the seasoned sea salt and bring to the boil.
Lower the heat and boil the potatoes for about 10 minutes until
just tender. Drain immediately and cool to room temperature.

Combine the garlic dressing and chopped rosemary. Thread
4 potatoes onto 1 or 2 kebab skewers each and insert a sprig of
rosemary on either end. Brush generously with the garlic
dressing mixture. Place under a grill or braai until nicely browned
and warmed through. Season with black pepper and serve.

COOK'S TIP
It is easier to use 2 kebab skewers when skewering anything,
it anchors the food and prevents it from slipping on the stick
when turning it on the braai.

SKEWERED LAMB CHOPS

SERVES 4

The problem with cooking chops under the grill or braai is
that the meat tends to overcook before the fat is crispy. This is
a brilliant way of cooking chops to perfection.

8–10 lamb loin chops
1 x Marinate-in-a-Bag, rosemary and mint flavour
8 kebab skewers

Place the chops in the bag and zip closed. First massage the
marinade into the meat for 1–2 minutes, then leave it to marinate
for 30 minutes at room temperature.

Remove the chops from the marinade with a pair of tongs and
thread 4–6 chops onto a kebab skewer through the meaty eye
of each chop. Push another skewer through, 1 cm away from the
first one, to stabilise the meat. Braai, with the fat-side down, over
medium heat until crisp, then turn and cook the meaty side.
Remove the chops from the sticks and lay them flat under the
grill or on the braai. Cook until nicely browned on the outside but
still slightly pink and juicy inside. Use any left-over marinade to
baste the chops while they are cooking.

HOME-MADE ROSEMARY
AND MINT MARINADE

½ cup (125 ml) olive oil
4 T (60 ml) lemon juice
2 t (10 ml) garlic and herb seasoning
4 T (60 ml) chopped fresh mint
2 T (30 ml) chopped fresh rosemary

Combine all the ingredients in a zip-lock plastic bag and use as
described above.

skewered lamb chops

BRAAIED BUTTERFLIED QUAILS

SERVES 6

*The quails may be butterflied and prepared with the seasoned
butter mixture a day in advance for convenience. Baby
chickens instead of quails are equally good.*

6 quails, butterflied
2 t (10 ml) garlic and herb seasoning
3 T (45 ml) butter, softened
1 T (15 ml) lemon juice
1 t (5 ml) chicken stock powder
6 spring onions with green parts, thinly sliced

To butterfly the quails, place a cleaned quail on a board, breast-
side down. Using a sharp knife or kitchen scissors, cut the quail
open along the backbone. Bend the cut ribs outwards and press
down firmly on the breast bone with the palm of your hand. The
quail will now be opened out flat (butterflied) beneath your hand.

Season the quails with the garlic and herb seasoning. Mix
together the butter, lemon juice, chicken stock powder and
sliced spring onions. Loosen the skin carefully over the breasts
and push the mixture in evenly under the skin, particularly over
the breast, to ensure it remains moist.

The quails can be prepared to this point a day in advance and
stored in the refrigerator. When you are ready to braai, place the
quails over the coals, skin side up, and cover with foil or an
inverted cast-iron pot to make a little oven. Alternatively, use a
kettle braai and cover with the lid. Braai for about 35 minutes
over moderate coals.

Serve with garlic bread and salad.

LAMB POTJIE WITH VEGETABLES

SERVES 6

*A perennial South African favourite. It allows plenty of time
to enjoy a few beers while it simmers away.*

2 kg lamb knuckles, cut into 3 cm pieces
1 cup (250 ml) chopped tomato
3 onions, chopped
3 T (45 ml) oil
2 cups (500 ml) chicken stock
4 t (20 ml) garlic and herb seasoning
500 g baby potatoes, halved
4 cloves garlic, cut into slithers lengthways
6 large carrots, sliced into thin rings
2 peppers (red and yellow), seeded and thickly sliced
1 small cauliflower, broken into florets
½ cup (125 ml) chopped parsley
250 g brown mushrooms
seasoned sea salt
freshly ground black pepper
4 T (60 ml) garlic butter

Combine the lamb and tomatoes and leave at room temperature
for 30 minutes. Sauté the onions in the oil. Add the lamb,
tomatoes, stock and the seasoning. Stir well and allow to
simmer for 1½ hours.

Layer the vegetables, garlic and parsley, in the order given in
the ingredients, on top of the meat. Season each layer as you
go. Place pats of garlic butter on top of the mushrooms. Cook
slowly without stirring for a further 30–45 minutes.

BLUE CHEESE BEEF BRAAI

SERVES 6

This recipe was adapted from one a friend
in America sent me – she called it Colonel's Steak.
The basting sauce combines some of the most unusual
flavours, but the end result is very good and meaty.
It is excellent served warm or at room temperature.

1.25 kg rolled and tied sirloin
1 t (5 ml) salt
1 t (5 ml) freshly ground black pepper
2 t (10 ml) beef stock powder
½ cup (125 ml) sour cream
4 T (60 ml) crumbled blue cheese
1 T (15 ml) good quality coffee granules
2 T (30 ml) boiling water

Rub the steak all over with the seasoning. Mix the dry beef stock powder and sour cream with the blue cheese. Dissolve the coffee granules in the boiling water and add it to the sauce. Marinate the meat in this delicious mixture for at least 3–4 hours, at room temperature.

Scrape off the excess marinade and use it to baste the meat during cooking. Any remaining sauce can be brought to the boil and served on the side at the table.

Baste and braai the meat very slowly, turning it regularly, until a meat thermometer inserted in the thickest part of the meat registers medium-rare (65 °C). Leave it to rest for 10 minutes before carving thinly.

Serve with country-style bread and a good selection of cheeses. A selection of grilled vegetables would satisfy non-meat eaters as well.

GINGER BEER

MAKES 3 LITRES

Nothing refreshes like this old-fashioned favourite.

2 cups (400 g) sugar
12 cups (3 litres) lukewarm water
1 t (5 ml) active dried yeast
1 t (5 ml) ground ginger
1 T (15 ml) grated fresh ginger

Dissolve the sugar in the lukewarm water. Add the yeast and ginger and mix well. Pour into bottles, leaving a bit of head space, and seal with corks or clingfilm. Leave to mature at room temperature for a day or two. Refrigerate before use.

COOK'S TIP
Do not seal the bottles with screw-in corks,
as the gas formed by the ginger beer
could cause the bottles to explode.

berry chocolate tart with pecan crust

'The components of a great dish are simplicity, elegance, graphic impact, texture and fine flavour.'

Marco Pierre White,

Harvey's Restaurant, London

DESSERT

BERRY CHOCOLATE TART
WITH PECAN CRUST

SERVES 6–8

A rich, pretty-looking tart. Change the berries
according to the season.

CRUST
1 cup (100 g) pecan nuts
10 tennis biscuits
4 T (60 ml) soft brown sugar
½ t (2.5 ml) ground cinnamon
4 T (60 ml) melted butter

FILLING
1 cup (250 ml) cream
200 g Albany dark chocolate, broken into squares
250 g cherries (stoned) or raspberries, or 500 g strawberries
4 T (60 ml) strawberry jam

Preheat the oven to 170 °C. Chop the pecan nuts and biscuits in a processor until crumbed. Add the sugar, cinnamon and melted butter. Pulse until blended and moist clumps form. Press the mixture up the sides and onto the base of a 22 cm spring form tin or a fluted porcelain flan dish. Bake for 25 minutes until golden and crispy. Leave to cool.

To make the filling, bring the cream just to the boil. Remove from the heat and pour slowly over the chocolate. Stir to melt the chocolate. Pour the mixture into the baked crust. Leave to set in the fridge for about 4 hours or overnight. Arrange the stoned cherries or berries over the top. Melt the jam over a low heat and brush over the fruit. Keep refrigerated.

COOK'S TIP
Brushing with jam is optional but essential when using strawberries.

FRESH AND DRIED
FRUIT SALAD WITH CITRUS CREAM

SERVES 8

This is one of the most refreshing and popular desserts we
have ever developed. A real South African winner.

125 g dried apricots, coarsely chopped
125 g dried mango, sliced into 1 cm lengths
125 g dried apple rings, coarsely chopped
1½ cups (375 ml) sparkling apple juice
500 g fresh, stoned litchis or 1 x 565 g tin litchis, drained
500 g strawberries or 250 g cherries, or 1 large bunch black grapes, halved and seeded

CITRUS CREAM
1 cup (250 ml) cream
pinch salt
¼ t (1 ml) ground cinnamon
¼ t (1 ml) ground ginger
2 T (30 ml) sugar
2 T (30 ml) orange liqueur or orange juice
2 t (10 ml) grated orange rind
½ cup (125 ml) plain yoghurt

Place the chopped dried fruit in the sparkling apple juice and soak for 3–4 hours or overnight in the fridge. Keep the litchis and strawberries, cherries or grapes in the fridge separately to be added just before serving.

To make the citrus cream, half whip the cream with the salt and spices. Add the sugar and whip until firm. Fold in the liqueur or orange juice, rind and yoghurt. Cover and chill.

FRESH BERRIES
WITH MERINGUE CREAM

SERVES 4–6

There is nothing nicer than the combination of berries, cream,
granadilla and meringue. Use ready-made meringues or
meringue nests. Assemble just before serving.

1 cup (250 ml) plain yoghurt
4 large meringues or meringue nests
1–1½ cups (250–375 ml) fresh berries (raspberries,
strawberries or blackcurrants)
3 granadillas
1 cup (250 ml) fresh cream
grated rind of half a lemon

Line a sieve with a layer of white absorbent paper towel and place it over a dish. Pour the yoghurt into the sieve and set it aside for at least half an hour to allow the excess moisture to drip through.

Break the meringues into approximately 1 cm pieces by placing them in a plastic bag and flattening them with the bottom of a saucepan or a rolling pin. Pick over the berries and rinse them, if necessary. Halve the granadillas and scoop out the pulp. Beat the cream until stiff. Mix the whipped cream with the yoghurt, half the granadilla pulp and all the lemon rind.

Just before serving, lightly mix the meringues and berries (reserving a few of the best for decoration) with the cream and spoon into pudding bowls. Pour over the remaining granadilla pulp and decorate with the reserved berries.

HONEYED FIGS

SERVES 4

This is a wonderful recipe to keep for the fig season;
it's quick, easy and absolutely delicious. I pour a little
Van der Hum over the figs just before serving.
Don't be stingy with the honey!

butter
about 8 large figs, peeled
4 T (60 ml) honey
250 g smooth cottage cheese or whipped cream
4 T (60 ml) Van der Hum liqueur (optional)

Melt enough butter to cover the base of a frying pan. Halve the figs lengthways and sauté them, cut side down, until golden brown. Turn from time to time. Drizzle the honey over the figs and heat to boiling point. Remove from the heat.

If you wish, pour the Van der Hum over just before serving, and serve hot or at room temperature with smooth cottage cheese, mascarpone or whipped cream.

DELUXE PEAR AND ALMOND TART

SERVES 10

A marvellous combination of nature's autumn bounty. It is important to blind-bake the pastry at a high temperature before adding the filling. Reduce the oven temperature after baking the pastry so as not to over-brown the filling. Delicious served with blue cheese.

SHORTCRUST PASTRY
1 cup (120 g) cake flour
pinch of salt
4 T (60 ml) butter, fridge temperature
1 egg yolk (reserve the white to brush over
the cooked pastry)
2–2½ T (30–40 ml) cold water

FILLING
1 cup (100 g) whole almonds or pecan nuts
½ cup (125 g) butter
½ cup (100 g) castor sugar
2 large eggs, separated
2 T (30 ml) flour
pinch salt
1 T (15 ml) Amaretto liqueur (optional) or
1 t (5 ml) vanilla essence
3 ripe pears
¼ cup (40 g) seedless raisins, rinsed with boiling water
and left to stand

To make the pastry, sift the flour and salt twice and rub in the butter to form coarse crumbs. Mix the egg yolk with cold water and add to the flour. Cut in the liquid with a small knife to form a lumpy mixture. Use your hand to gather and knead the mixture together until it forms a ball. Don't add more water, simply keep working the dough lightly. Wrap the dough in plastic and leave it to rest (in cooler weather, it is best to leave it out of the fridge, as it can become too hard and brittle).

Roll the dough out to 1 cm thickness. Fold into thirds and roll out again to 3 mm thickness on a well-floured surface, using a floured rolling pin. (The preliminary rolling makes the dough much easier to handle.) Use the pastry to line a 20–22 cm loose-bottomed flan tin. Rest the unbaked pastry open in the fridge, for at least 30 minutes, to firm and dry out slightly.

Preheat the oven to 200 °C. Line the pastry case with greaseproof paper and weigh down with rice or beans. Bake blind (without filling) for 10 minutes. Remove the paper and the weight. Brush the hot pastry with the lightly beaten egg white to form a 'waterproof' layer between the pastry and the filling. Allow the pastry to cool.

Turn the oven down to 160 °C. Place the nuts in a processor and chop them up until they resemble breadcrumbs.

Cream the butter, add the sugar and continue creaming until light and fluffy. Add the eggs slowly, first the white and then the yolk of each egg, beating vigorously between additions.

Mix the flour and salt with the ground nuts and fold into the creamed mixture. Fold in the liqueur or vanilla.

Peel the pears, slice into halves and remove the pips. Slice each half into slices. Fan the sliced pear halves in the baked pastry case. Sprinkle over the raisins. Spoon over the topping and smooth evenly. Bake at 160 °C for about 45 minutes, until it is a rich golden brown colour. Serve warm or at room temperature with creamed cottage cheese, or with slices of blue cheese.

CREAMED COTTAGE CHEESE
½ cup (125 ml) fresh cream
125 g smooth cottage cheese

Whip the cream until it holds its shape, then fold it into the cottage cheese.

deluxe pear and almond tart

PEARS BAKED
WITH MARSALA AND CINNAMON

SERVES 6

*A perennial favourite, especially during the cold
winter months.*

6 ripe pears
3 T (45 ml) butter, at room temperature
½ cup (120 g) soft brown sugar
¾ cup (180 ml) Marsala, or any sweet red wine
4 T (60 ml) white wine or white Vermouth
2 cinnamon sticks, roughly broken
crème fraîche or whipped cream

Preheat the oven to 180 °C. Cut a small slice from the rounded
end of each pear so that it will stand up, then remove the core,
working from the base. Brush a little soft butter over the skin of
each pear and stand them in an ovenproof dish. Dust the pears
with sugar. Pour in the Marsala and white wine at the side of the
dish. Break and scatter the cinnamon sticks over the pears, then
cover the dish loosely with wet greaseproof paper. Bake for
about 45 minutes, until the pears are very tender and slightly
shrivelled. Serve warm with their juices and crème fraîche or
whipped cream.

CRÈME FRAÎCHE
2 T (30 ml) buttermilk
½ cup (125 ml) cream

To make your own crème fraîche, mix together the buttermilk
and cream and leave to stand at room temperature overnight.
(Alternatively, use a shop-bought variety.)

DELUXE SAGO
PUDDING WITH APRICOT SAUCE

SERVES 8

*Rich and fattening, but divine. Treat yourself to this
old-fashioned favourite at least once every winter.*

½ cup (125 ml) sago
1 cup (250 ml) full cream milk
1 cup (250 ml) cream
pinch of salt
1 x 397 g tin sweetened full cream condensed milk
½ t (2.5 ml) baking powder
2 large eggs, separated
⅓ cup (80 g) soft brown sugar
1½ t (7.25 ml) ground cinnamon

APRICOT SAUCE
½ cup (85 g) dried apricots
¾ cup (180 ml) water
3 T (45 ml) sugar
4 T (60 ml) sweet sherry
1 t (5 ml) grated orange peel

Simmer the sago very slowly for 30 minutes in a mixture of the
milk and cream with a pinch of salt. Meanwhile, butter 8 ramekin
dishes or a medium-sized ovenproof dish.

Preheat the oven to 200 °C. Remove the sago from the heat.
Leave to cool to touch temperature. Add the condensed milk,
baking powder and egg yolks and mix in. Whip the egg whites
until soft peaks form and fold gently into the mixture. Dish into
the prepared ramekins or ovenproof dish. Mix together the sugar
and cinnamon and sprinkle over the pudding. Bake for about
20–30 minutes until puffy and nicely browned.

To make the apricot sauce, simmer the apricots in the water
until soft, then sweeten them with the sugar. Purée the fruit. Add
the sherry and orange peel and season with a tiny pinch of salt.
Serve the pudding hot, with the apricot sauce.

GRAPEFRUIT ALASKA

SERVES 6

This is a real party piece. Put sparklers into the individual Alaskas and carry them to the table with stars shooting – remember to dim the lights! Prepare and measure everything for the meringue; it takes a few minutes just before serving

3 pink grapefruit
2 T (30 ml) sugar
2 T (30 ml) orange liqueur
6 scoops vanilla or berry ice cream

MERINGUE TOPPING
3 egg whites
½ t (2.5 ml) cider vinegar or lemon juice
¾ cup (150 g) castor sugar

Cut the grapefruit in half. Remove the segments with a grapefruit knife or spoon. Squeeze out the juice and reserve. Scrape all the fibrous membranes neatly out of the shells.

Toss the grapefruit segments with the sugar and liqueur. Add a little juice to keep them moist, then divide the segments between the 6 grapefruit-skin halves. Keep the halves steady and level in a muffin pan. Place a large scoop of ice cream on top of the fruit. Store in the freezer.

The meringue is best made at the last minute, piped over and flash baked in a hot oven just before serving.

Heat the oven to 250 °C or turn on the grill. To make the meringue, beat the egg whites until foaming lightly, then add the white vinegar. Use an electric beater and a glass bowl, or a metal whisk and a copper bowl, but never a plastic bowl (the oil in the plastic prevents the egg white from foaming). Continue beating until the mixture is thick, stiff and slightly dry. Gradually add the castor sugar, spoonful by spoonful, beating continuously, until the meringue becomes thick and shiny. Spoon the meringue mixture into a piping bag fitted with a large star nozzle. Pipe the meringue over the ice cream, going right down to the edges of the grapefruit, to form a heat-proof seal.

Bake the grapefruit for 5-10 minutes until the meringue is crispy and tinged with brown, or flash them under a hot grill. You can also colour the meringue with a small cook's blow torch. Serve immediately.

QUINCE AND APPLE CRUMBLE

SERVES 6–8

1 kg quinces
1½ cups (300 g) sugar
¾ cup (180 ml) water
750 g Granny Smith apples
1 cup (120 g) cake flour
¾ cup (150 g) castor sugar
100 g butter, cut into cubes

Peel and core the quinces and cut them into wedges. Place the quinces in a pot with sugar and water and simmer until they are just tender.

Peel and core the apples and cut into wedges. Add to the quinces and mix together. Simmer without a lid for another 10 minutes until the apples are just tender.

Preheat the oven to 180 °C. In a medium-sized bowl mix together the flour and castor sugar. Rub in the butter with your fingers until the mixture resembles coarse breadcrumbs.

Spoon the fruit into a medium-sized baking dish and spread the crumbed mixture evenly over the fruit.

Bake for 30 minutes or until the topping is golden brown. Serve warm with custard or cream.

VARIATION
Use pears if quinces are not available.

BLUE CHEESE
WITH DATES AND WALNUTS

125 g creamy blue cheese, crumbled
125 g ricotta cheese or smooth cottage cheese
½ cup (125 ml) cream
125 g dates
1 cup (100 g) walnuts or pecan nuts
1 T (15 ml) butter
sweet digestive biscuits

Combine the blue cheese with the ricotta or cottage cheese. Whip the cream until it holds its shape, then fold it into the cheese mixture. Line a small pudding bowl with muslin or white kitchen paper towel. Spoon the mixture into the bowl and refrigerate. Separate the dates and toast the nuts in the butter.

Turn out the cheese mould and peel away the cloth or paper. Arrange the nuts, dates and digestive biscuits on the side.

PEARS WITH
BLUE CHEESE AND CREAM

SERVES 4

Easy as pie and quite divine! It looks lovely decorated with violas or blue pansies.

2 ripe pears, skinned, halved and pips removed
125 g creamy blue cheese
½ cup (125 ml) fresh cream

Preheat the oven to 200 °C. Butter 4 small ovenproof dishes. Slice the pears and fan the halves in the dishes. Crumble the blue cheese over the pears and spoon over the cream. Bake for 20 minutes.

BEST EVER PARTY-SIZE TIRAMISU

SERVES 16

There are many variations on this theme, but this is one of the best.

4 t (20 ml) good quality coffee granules
2 T (30 ml) boiling water
1½ cups (375 ml) cream
250 g mascarpone cheese
4 T (60 ml) sweetened condensed milk
150 g Albany dark chocolate, melted
250 g sponge fingers (about 45 biscuits)
1 cup (250 ml) coffee liqueur
50 g Albany dark chocolate, melted

Dissolve the coffee granules in the boiling water. Leave to cool. Whip the cream until stiff and blend in the mascarpone, condensed milk, melted chocolate and cooled coffee. Toss the biscuits in the liqueur. Layer the biscuits and the chocolate mixture in a rectangular dish. Decorate the dessert with melted chocolate. Refrigerate the tiramisu overnight or for a couple of hours before serving.

COOK'S TIP

Smooth cottage cheese may be used if mascarpone is not available. Don't leave out the condensed milk – I came across this touch in an excellent restaurant in Italy known for its tiramisu.

best ever party-size tiramisu

pear cake with raisins

'Love and eggs are best when

they are fresh.'

Unknown

BAKING

AMERICAN-STYLE LIME AND LEMON CHEESECAKE

SERVES 12

This fridge cheese cake is outstanding. Serve it in the summer to round off a garden buffet spread or in the winter decorated with edible flowers.

CRUST
1¼ cups (310 ml) crushed tennis biscuits (about 20 biscuits)
1 t (5 ml) ground cinnamon
6 T (90 ml) melted butter

FILLING
1 T (15 ml) gelatine
2 T (30 ml) water
250 g smooth cottage cheese
1 cup (250 ml) plain yoghurt
1 x 397 tin sweetened condensed milk
2 T (30 ml) lime cordial
4 T (60 ml) lemon juice
1 t (5 ml) vanilla essence

TOPPING
1 cup (250 ml) cream
1 T (15 ml) sugar
½ t (2.5 ml) gelatine
2 t (10 ml) grated lemon rind
pinch of salt

Preheat the oven to 190 °C. To make the crust, crumb the biscuits, add the cinnamon and bind it with the melted butter. Press the crumbed mixture onto the bottom of a 22 cm pie plate. Bake for about 10–15 minutes to crisp and brown lightly. Leave to cool.

Sprinkle the gelatine over the water and leave it to sponge. Beat the cottage cheese and yoghurt with the condensed milk, and add the lime and lemon juice and vanilla essence. Melt the gelatine in the microwave for about 30 seconds on high and add it to the mixture. Beat to mix everything thoroughly. Taste and add a little more lemon if it is too sweet. Pour the filling into the prepared crust. Refrigerate.

Half whip the cream. Mix the sugar, dry gelatine, lemon rind and salt together and beat them into the cream until it holds soft peaks. Spread or pipe the flavoured cream over the pie. Refrigerate until serving time, preferably overnight.

Decorate with lime and lemon zest as illustrated on page 117.

COOK'S TIP
The cheesecake can also be prepared in a 20 cm springform cake tin. Line the base with baking paper and place the crumb mixture on the base only. Spoon the filling over and top with the cream. Release the tin only once the cake has set. It must be left overnight in the fridge.

EASY ALMOND, RICOTTA AND HONEY CHEESECAKE

SERVES 6–8

The ingredients in this recipe – ricotta, almonds, lemon and honey – are quintessentially Sicilian. What makes this version special is that unblanched almonds are used, so that the baked filling is flecked with brown and almond-laden in flavour.
We have simplified the preparation so you get a superb result with minimum time invested.
If you are serving it as a dessert, it is excellent with red wine sauce.

CRUST
1 packet (125 g) sponge fingers, crushed
4 T (60 ml) melted butter

1 cup (100 g) unblanched almonds
500 g fresh ricotta cheese
3 extra large eggs
6 T (90 ml) honey
2 t (10 ml) custard powder
¼ cup (50 g) castor sugar
pinch of salt
finely grated zest of half a medium lemon
2 T (30 ml) lemon juice
½ cup (125 ml) cream, lightly whipped
1 t (5 ml) vanilla essence

Preheat the oven to 160 °C.

Spread the crushed biscuits into the base of a porcelain flan dish 22–25 cm in diameter. Drizzle the melted butter over as evenly as you can. Don't mix; it will bind as it bakes.

Process the unblanched almonds to a mealie meal consistency. Beat the ricotta until smooth with an electric hand beater, then beat in the eggs one at a time, followed by the honey, custard powder, sugar, salt, lemon zest and juice. Fold in the cream, vanilla and ground almonds.

Pour the mixture over the biscuit base. Bake for about 30–40 minutes, until set. Serve warm or at room temperature.

VARIATION
Smooth cottage cheese can be used as a substitute for ricotta.

RED WINE SAUCE
1 cup (200 g) sugar
1 cup (250 ml) red wine
3 cloves
¼ t (1 ml) black pepper
strips of lemon rind

Combine the ingredients and boil for 15 minutes until thickened and reduced. Serve hot or cold.

APPLE TART WITH BOILED CONDENSED MILK

SERVES 6–8

This is one of my husband's absolute favourites.

1 x 397 g tin sweetened full cream condensed milk, boiled (not the bought variety)
4 Granny Smith apples, peeled, cored and sliced
2 T (30 ml) honey or soft brown sugar
1 t (5 ml) ground cinnamon
1 t (5 ml) grated lemon rind
juice of half a lemon
pinch of salt
4 T (60 ml) water

TOPPING
½ cup (45 g) instant oats
¼ cup (60 g) soft brown sugar
¼ cup (30 g) cake flour
pinch of salt
5 T (75 g) butter
½ cup (50 g) pecan nuts, coarsely chopped

Boil the tin of condensed milk in a saucepan, with just enough water to cover the tin, for 55 minutes over moderate heat. Allow the tin to cool off before opening it, or hot condensed milk could spurt out. Preheat the oven to 180 °C. Meanwhile, mix the apples with the sugar, cinnamon, lemon rind, lemon juice and salt. Spoon into a 25–28 cm diameter pie plate. Pour in the water carefully at the side of the dish. Drop spoonfuls of the boiled condensed milk over and spread out evenly with the back of a dessert spoon.

To make the topping, mix together the oats, sugar, flour and salt. Rub in the butter with your fingertips to make a crumbly mixture. Add the chopped pecan nuts and sprinkle the mixture over the tart. Bake for 45 minutes until nicely browned. Serve hot or at room temperature with vanilla ice cream or whipped cream.

GREEN FIG TART WITH NUTS

SERVES 6–8

This recipe has really stood the test of time. A lecturer of mine, Dr Ina Strassheim, taught me the secrets of this tart during my student years.

CRUMB CRUST
1 cup (250 ml) ground Marie biscuit crumbs
4 T (60 ml) melted butter

FILLING
3 extra large eggs, separated
¾ cup (150 g) white sugar
1 x 410 g tin evaporated milk
1 T (15 ml) gelatine
4 T (60 ml) cold water
1 cup (100 g) chopped pecan nuts
1 t (5 ml) almond essence
1 cup (250 ml) diced green figs in syrup

Preheat the oven to 180 °C. Mix the biscuit crumbs with the melted butter, adding a little lemon juice if the mixture is too dry. Press the crust mixture to a thickness of about 2 mm into a pie plate, using a spoon. Bake for 10 minutes. Alternatively, leave unbaked and chill in the refrigerator until firm.

Beat the egg yolks and the sugar together. Heat the milk and add it to the egg yolks. Place the mixture in a double boiler over boiling water and stir until thickened. Sprinkle the gelatine over cold water and soak for 5 minutes, then stir it into the hot custard mixture. Add the nuts, almond essence and diced green figs and allow to cool until the mixture starts to set. Whisk the egg whites until stiff and fold them into the mixture. Pour into the crumb crust and chill.

VARIATION
Use glacé green figs instead of fig preserve.

PEAR CAKE WITH RAISINS

SERVES 8

This is a special cake – rich and fruity.

CARAMELISED FRUIT
100 g butter
4 large ripe pears, peeled and cored
4 T (60 ml) honey
pinch of salt
½ cup (85 g) seedless raisins

CAKE MIXTURE
250 g butter
250 g icing sugar
4 extra large eggs
½ t (2.5 ml) salt
1 T (15 ml) baking powder
2¼ cups (270 g) cake flour
4 T (60 ml) brandy or fresh orange juice

Cut the pears into 1 cm cubes. Melt the butter in a large, heavybased frying pan over high heat and sauté the diced pears in the butter until nicely browned. Add the honey, salt and raisins and cook until a brown caramel sauce forms. Allow to cool.

Preheat the oven to 180 °C. Grease a 22 cm diameter round, springform tin and line the base well with greased baking or butter paper.

Beat the butter and the icing sugar until light and creamy. Add the eggs, one at a time – first the white and then the yolk of each egg. Beat well after each addition.

Sift the dry ingredients twice. Fold the dry mixture into the creamed mixture alternately with the brandy or orange juice. Fold in the cooled pears until just mixed. Spoon the mixture into the prepared pan. Bake for about 50 minutes. Allow to cool.

Serve, thinly sliced, with coffee.

ORANGE AND ALMOND CAKE

MAKES 1 SINGLE-LAYER CAKE

I found this interesting recipe in Australia. It's economical for those lucky enough to have an almond tree in the garden. The orange is cooked whole and then mixed with the rest of the ingredients in the food processor, a method which produces a marvellous orange flavour. The entire cake can be mixed in a food processor.

2 whole, unpeeled oranges
1 cup (250 ml) water
2½ cups (250 g) blanched almonds
1 cup (200 g) castor sugar
2 T (30 ml) cornflour
1 t (5 ml) baking powder
½ t (2.5 ml) salt
6 large eggs
1 t (5 ml) vanilla essence
icing sugar

Boil the whole oranges slowly for 1½ hours in the water. This can be done a day in advance.

Preheat the oven to 200 °C. Grease a deep baking tin 20 cm in diameter with butter. Place the almonds, castor sugar, cornflour, baking powder and salt in a food processor and chop the almonds until they resemble coarsely ground breadcrumbs.

Quarter the cooled, cooked oranges (peel and all), remove any pips, and add it to the almond mixture. Now add the eggs, one at a time. Add the vanilla essence. Mix in a food processor.

Spoon the mixture into the tin and bake for 1 hour until golden brown and firm. Sift the icing sugar over just before serving. Serve with whipped cream.

EASTER CAKE WITH ALMONDS

SERVES 10–12

I like the rich, dense texture of this flat, flavoursome almond cake. The cake rises very little, so don't judge it by its appearance!

200 ml (115 g) ground almonds
1 cup (160 g) icing sugar
200 ml (100 g) cake flour
1 t (5 ml) baking powder
½ t (2.5 ml) salt
3 extra large egg yolks
½ cup (125 ml) melted butter, cooled
½ t (2.5 ml) almond essence

ICING
1½ cups (240 g) icing sugar
1 T (15 ml) boiling water
½ T (7.5 ml) lemon juice

DECORATION
whole almonds
strips of lemon rind

Preheat the oven to 170 °C. Grease a deep 22 cm x 5 cm cake tin well with butter and line the base with a circle of baking parchment or greased butter paper. Mix the almonds, icing sugar, flour, baking powder and salt lightly with your fingers in a mixing bowl, or sift it through a coarse sieve or colander. Make a hollow in the centre of the flour mixture and add the egg yolks, cooled melted butter and the almond essence. Stir with a small wooden spoon until the ingredients are well mixed.

Spread the mixture out in the prepared cake tin and lightly press it flat. Make a slight hollow in the centre and drop the tin once or twice from a height of 10 cm from the work surface to allow the air bubbles to escape. Bake for 35–40 minutes. The cake should be slightly moist.

Allow the cake to cool for at least 15 minutes in the tin, then turn it out carefully onto a wire rack. Allow to cool completely.

Sift the icing sugar into a bowl and mix it to a thick, smooth paste with the boiling water and lemon juice. Add more liquid if the mixture is too stiff to spread. Decorate the flattest side of the cake. Use a palette knife dipped in boiling water to spread the icing smoothly. Decorate with whole almonds and strips of lemon rind. Serve in thin slices with coffee.

MOIST BUTTERNUT HEALTH BREAD

MAKES 1 LARGE OR 8 MINI LOAVES

This recipe comes from Cheryl Graham, who heads up the
Pick 'n Pay cookery school in Claremont, Cape Town.
We have worked together for many years and I hold Cheryl's
skills, drive and love of food in high regard.
Toasting the sunflower seeds is important, otherwise they tend
to turn green when combined with the bicarbonate of soda.
Just shake them in a frying pan with a little oil until
golden and crispy.

½ cup (75 g) sunflower seeds, toasted
3 cups (420 g) wholewheat flour
1 t (5 ml) bicarbonate of soda
1 T (15 ml) baking powder
1 t (5 ml) salt
1 cup (42 g) All Bran flakes, lightly crushed
1 cup (250 ml) grated, raw butternut
3 T (45 ml) honey
1 extra large egg, beaten
2 cups (500 ml) buttermilk
about ½ cup (125 ml) water

Preheat the oven to 180 °C. Combine the first seven ingredients. Beat the honey, egg, buttermilk and water together and add to the dry ingredients. Mix well to form a sticky bread dough. Spoon into a large buttered loaf tin or 8 mini loaf tins and bake for about 1 hour for a large loaf, or 40 minutes for the smaller loaves. Serve with a savoury dip or spread.

CAPE-STYLE WHOLEWHEAT BREAD

A nice, quick-mix bread that requires no kneading.
The vitamin C keeps the bread moist.

1 cup (200 g) crushed wheat
3 cups (420 g) wholewheat bread flour
1½ t (7.5 ml) salt
1 x 10 g packet instant dried yeast
1 cup (120 g) white bread flour
1 cup (42 g) All Bran flakes
2 T (30 ml) skim milk powder
4 T (60 ml) molasses or treacle
1 T (15 ml) oil
1 x water soluble Vitamin C tablet (optional)
about 2½ cups (625 ml) lukewarm water
½ cup (75 g) sunflower seeds

Preheat the oven to 220 °C. Mix the dry ingredients. Add the molasses or treacle and oil. Dissolve the Vitamin C tablet in the water and add to the dry ingredients, together with sunflower seeds, stirring well. Pour the dough into a well-greased loaf tin (22 x 12 x 6 cm). Leave to rise in a warm place for 30 minutes. Bake for 35 minutes. Remove the bread from the tin and bake for a further 5–7 minutes in the oven to crisp the bottom crust.

JESSIE'S BISCUITS

MAKES ABOUT 100 BISCUITS

*This is a great recipe for children who are always starving
and insist that there's never anything to eat in the house!
It's also a great lunch-box filler.
My friend Janet's 8-year-old daughter, Jessie, loves to help her
mother bake and this is one of her favourites. Jessie says one
can use rice crispies instead of cornflakes.*

250 g butter
2 cups (400 g) sugar
2 eggs
1 t (5 ml) vanilla essence
2 T (30 ml) peanut butter (crunchy or smooth)
2 t (10 ml) bicarbonate of soda
⅓ cup (80 ml) milk
2 cups (240 g) cake flour
2 t (10 ml) baking powder
½ t (2.5 ml) salt
2 cups (160 g) desiccated coconut
2 cups (180 g) rolled oats
2 cups (85 g) cornflakes

Preheat the oven to 180 °C. Cream together the butter and
sugar until light and fluffy. Add the eggs one at a time and beat
in. Beat in the vanilla and peanut butter. Add the bicarb to the
milk, stir well then stir into the creamed mixture. Sift together the
flour, baking powder and salt and fold into the mixture. Stir well.
Stir in the coconut, oats and lastly the cornflakes. Roll into
walnut-sized balls. Place on a greased baking tray, not too close
together. Do not flatten. Bake for 10–12 minutes or until golden
brown in colour. Allow to cool on a cooling rack, then store in an
airtight container.

CRUSTLESS MILK TART

MAKES 2 X 20 CM TARTS OR 1 LARGE 30 CM TART

*Few of us can resist a slice of fluffy milk tart, rich with butter
and aromatic spices. By not making a crust, you will save
time – and more than a few kilojoules.*

4 cups (1 litre) milk
½ stick cinnamon
rind of ½ lemon or orange
3 T (45 ml) butter
1 cup (120 g) bread flour
1 cup (200 g) sugar
¼ t (1 ml) salt
1½ t (7.5 ml) baking powder
4 eggs, separated
½ t (2.5 ml) almond essence
about 2 t (10 ml) ground cinnamon

Bring milk, cinnamon, rind and butter to the boil. Remove from
heat and leave to draw for 20 minutes. Mix flour, sugar, salt and
baking powder. Strain milk and add it to egg yolks, then beat this
mixture into flour mixture. Add almond essence. Return mixture
to stove and bring to the boil over medium heat, stirring with a
wooden spoon. (Don't despair if a few lumps form – just beat
them out with the beater after you have whipped the egg whites.)

Butter pie plates generously with soft butter and dust with
bread, biscuit or rusk crumbs (or use oats, muesli or whatever is
available). Whip egg whites with a drop of vinegar or lemon juice
until they hold their shape and form soft peaks. Beat tart mixture
to remove lumps. Fold egg white into tart mixture and pour into
pie plates. Dust with the cinnamon. Bake for 25–35 minutes at
190 °C. Switch off oven and leave to cool for 15 minutes in warm
oven. Serve hot or at room temperature.

crustless milk tart

janet's apricot jam

'Time may be a great healer, but it's a

lousy beautician.'

The Wanderer

P R E S E R V E S

Janet Hacking, a friend and colleague, wrote this chapter. She has access to fruit from her family farm in Citrusdal, and regularly makes jams and chutneys. I have known Janet for many years, since she was a Home Economics student at the Cape Technikon, and applaud her success as a demonstrator, teacher and food selector.

HINTS FOR PRESERVING

- Use a large, heavybased preserving pan to prevent burning. It should be wide enough to allow for evaporation and deep enough to prevent the jam from boiling over.

- Use a long-handled wooden spoon for stirring, as this will help prevent hot jam from splashing onto your hands.

- The jars used for bottling should be thoroughly washed. Dry them by placing them on a baking sheet in the oven at 150 °C for 20 minutes. (This will also sterilise them.) Wash the screw tops and sterilise them in boiling water. The jars may be sealed with waxed paper discs or melted wax.

- How to test whether marmalade or jam is set: A sugar thermometer may be used to determine the setting point, which is 105 °C. Another way to test if it is ready is to drop 5 ml onto a chilled plate, allow it to cool in the freezer for 5 minutes and to push the mixture to one side with your finger. If the skin wrinkles, it has reached setting point.

- Pectin is the substance in fruit that reacts with the fruit acids when heated and sets the jam. It is a good idea to add extra pectin when the fruit is slightly overripe and therefore deficient in natural pectin. Dissolve the pectin in a little brandy or whisky (it is easier to dissolve pectin in alcohol than in water) and add it to the boiling fruit. One teaspoon for every kilogram of fruit is normally sufficient. Pectin can be bought at pharmacies.

- Always use fresh ingredients of the best quality available. Do not use overripe or green fruit and vegetables.

- Never add sugar too soon, as it toughens the fruit.

- Remove any scum that may develop with a stainless steel slotted spoon once the jam is ready rather than during cooking, as this is wasteful.

JANET'S APRICOT JAM

MAKES 6–8 x 400 G JARS

The apricot kernels, prepared as described here, give the jam a lovely almond flavour. The amount of sugar added depends on how sweet you like the jam.

2 kg stoned ripe apricots
3 lemons
2½–3 kg white sugar
½ cup (125 ml) apricot kernels

Wash the apricots before cutting them in half and stoning them. Weigh. Roughly chop them in a processor if you want a smoother jam. Place the fruit in a heavybased saucepan.

Cut the lemons in half and remove the pips with a fork. Squeeze out the juice and add it to the fruit, together with the lemon halves. (This helps with the pectin development.)

Bring the fruit to the boil and cook for about 15 minutes, until the apricots are soft. Add the sugar and heat slowly, until all the sugar has dissolved. It is very important not to boil the jam until all the sugar has dissolved. Boil rapidly (this will give the jam a light, clear colour). Stir occasionally.

While the jam is cooking, prepare the apricot kernels. Crack open the pips with a nutcracker or hammer. Remove the kernels and place them in a small bowl. Pour over boiling water to loosen the skins and then peel them off.

Test the jam after it has cooked for about 20–30 minutes to see whether it has reached setting point (see Hints above). When it is done, remove the jam from the stove, squeeze out the lemon halves and remove them. Add the kernels and stir through slowly.

Bottle while still hot in warm, dry, sterilised jars. Cover with wax paper dipped in brandy or melted wax before screwing on the lids. Label and store in a cool, dry place.

JANET'S
MICROWAVE STRAWBERRY JAM

MAKES 1½ X 400 G JARS

This jam is best made in the microwave as the strawberries remain whole, and the entire process takes only 18–20 minutes. End-of-season strawberries are cheaper and still make very good jam. An equal amount of sugar as fruit may be added for a sweeter result. Mulberries or youngberries can be used in the same way.

500 g strawberries
2 T (30 ml) lemon juice
350 g sugar

Grease the inside rim of a large, microwave-proof bowl with a little butter to prevent the jam from boiling over.

Wash and then hull the strawberries, keeping them whole. Place them in the bowl with the lemon juice. Without covering the bowl, microwave on high (100 per cent) for 3 minutes. Add the sugar and stir well. Microwave on high for a further 5 minutes. Stir and scrape down the sides of the bowl. Microwave on high for a further 10 minutes, stopping and stirring occasionally.

Test for setting point (see Hints on page 124). If it is still too runny, cook it for a further 2 minutes.

Bottle while hot in warm, dry, sterilised jars. Cover with wax paper dipped in brandy or melted wax before screwing on the lid. Label and store in a cool, dry place.

JOAN DEWING'S
GREEN FIG PRESERVE

MAKES 5 X 400 G JARS

Joan gave me this treasured recipe about a year before her untimely death. Like the beautiful flowers Joan arranged, I am sure it will bring pleasure to many. Her secret was to cut the crosses in the figs only after they have been boiled and are soft. In this way they absorb the syrup and become heavy and juicy.

1.5 kg figs
4 T (60 ml) salt
8 cups (2 litres) water
clean, fresh water

SUGAR SYRUP
2 kg sugar
12 cups (3 litres) water
2 x 3 cm pieces fresh ginger, peeled

juice of 1 lemon, strained

Scrape the figs with a sharp knife to remove the surface skin. Mix the salt and water and leave the figs overnight in this.

Bring a pot of clean, fresh water to the boil. Add the figs, cover with a thick 'blanket' of fig leaves and boil uncovered for no longer than about 15 minutes, until tender when tested with a toothpick. (The leaves add flavour and preserve the colour.) .

While the figs are boiling, prepare the sugar syrup. Add the ginger to the syrup.

Rinse the figs under cold water as soon as they are tender and cut a deep cross in the flower end of each fig. Add the softened figs to the boiling syrup and cook slowly in an open pan for about 1½–2 hours, until the figs are glossy and well impregnated with syrup. The syrup should begin to thicken. Add the strained lemon juice half an hour before the figs are ready.

Bottle while hot in sterilised jam jars.

BLACK OLIVES IN BRINE

This is an Old Cape method for bottling olives.
Use olives that have changed colour but are not overripe.
The whole process takes several weeks.

olives
300 g salt
20 cups (5 litres) water
cider or malt vinegar
bay leaves
lemon slices
olive oil

Using a razor blade, slit each olive from base to apex (a knife makes too wide a slit). Place the olives in a large container (I use a large plastic bucket), and cover them with tap water. Allow to stand for 4 weeks, changing the water once a day by tipping the bucket, pouring off the old water and replacing it with fresh.

After 4 weeks, make the brine by adding the salt to the water in the proportions given, depending on the quantity of olives you have. Pour the water off the olives and cover them with brine. (You can leave the olives in the bucket if you have a large quantity, or soak them in brine in jars if you have a lesser quantity.) Allow them to stand for 1 week in the brine.

Wash the olives in fresh water and then leave them to stand in enough vinegar to cover them for 3–4 hours. Pour off the vinegar. Bottle in sterilised jars using fresh brine. Add a bay leaf and lemon slice to each bottle. For variation you could add a chilli, garlic clove, coriander seeds or fresh herbs, such as a sprig of rosemary.

Pour enough olive oil into each jar to cover the surface of the brine. Seal the jars and leave them to stand preferably for a few weeks before use.

JANET'S SEVILLE ORANGE MARMALADE

MAKES 8–9 X 400 G JARS

Use the oranges as soon as possible after they have been picked. This ensures that the fruit is rich in pectin. If you don't have time to make the marmalade straight away, the oranges can be frozen whole and used to make marmalade at a later date.
I use a food processor to chop up the fruit, but for a less chunky marmalade the skins may also be thinly sliced by hand. Obviously the amount of marmalade you make is dependent on the amount of oranges and lemons available, but the proportions are as follows:

4 large Seville oranges
2 large lemons
8 cups (2 litres) water
white sugar (1 part sugar to 1 part fruit pulp)

Thinly peel the oranges and lemons. Place the outer peel in a food processor and chop it up to the desired coarseness, or slice finely by hand.

Peel the pith from the fruit and place the pith, together with the pips, into a muslin bag. Tie it up loosely. (This supplies the pectin.) Coarsly chop the flesh of the oranges and lemons.

Put the peel and flesh into a large, heavybased saucepan, together with the muslin bag and the water. Bring to the boil and simmer gently until the volume has reduced by one-third and the fruit is soft. Squeeze out the muslin bag and discard.

Measure the cooked pulp, then return it to the pan with an equal amount of sugar. Stir over a gentle heat until the sugar has dissolved, then boil for about 1 hour until setting point is reached (see Hints on page 124).

Allow to cool for 2–3 minutes so that the fruit can be evenly distributed. Pour into warm, sterilised jars. Cover with melted wax and seal.

janet's seville orange marmalade

index

index

index